Jesus, Lamb of God

Jesus, Lamb of God

BIBLICAL MEDITATIONS

David Atkinson

SPCK

First published 1996
The Society for Promoting Christian Knowledge
Holy Trinity Church
Marylebone Road
London
NW1 4DU

Bible quotations are from the *New International Version,*
copyright © 1973, 1978, 1984 *by the International Bible
Society.* Published by Hodder & Stoughton.

British Library Cataloguing in Publication Data
A catalogue record for this book is available from the British Library.

ISBN 0-281-04911-4

Typeset by Acorn Bookwork, Salisbury, Wilts
Printed in Great Britain by Biddles Ltd., Guildford and King's Lynn

Contents

for friends and colleagues
at Wycliffe Hall, Oxford

Introduction

I vividly remember visiting my mother's cousin's house in Beckenham. Her aged father lived there with her. The most fascinating thing about the visit to me, a young boy of eight or nine, and to my younger brother, was our great uncle's lantern-slide projector. He had made it out of an old wooden orange box, with metal tubes and glass lenses, a mirror and an electric light bulb. There was a compartment into which we could put a painted glass plate. When the light shined through the plate, the picture painted on it was projected on to the white wall of the room. This was an early home-made version of the slide projectors which were to become much more common a few years later when colour photography progressed to transparencies. But as I remember it now, it was much more fun. And the most fun thing of all was for my brother and me to take several glass picture slides and put them all into the projector at the same time, so that the light shone through them all together. Then the image on the wall was a composite picture made up of several different slides.

I find this an interesting way of depicting the composite pictures sometimes used in the New Testament to describe Jesus Christ: they are often made up of several different and apparently unconnected earlier pictures from the Old Testament. This, I believe, is what we find going on when, for example, John the

Baptist in the first chapter of the Fourth Gospel points to Jesus and says 'Behold! the Lamb of God.'

In many ways that was a most unexpected and unexplained phrase. Yet if we understand it as a composite picture made up of several different glass slides picked out of different parts of the Old Testament and early Jewish literature, and allow the light to shine through all of them together, we can begin to see some of the richness and relevance of John the Baptist's chosen expression.

Things had been very out of the ordinary when John was born. His father had been a priest. Priests ought to believe God, no doubt, but Zechariah had found it difficult to believe the angel's word that his wife Elizabeth would have a son (Luke 1.5ff.). They were both fairly old, long past the age for children. However, a son was born, and (to the surprise of the neighbours who thought he should be called after his father) was named John. John grew up in the hill country of Judah where, so far as we can tell, he lived for about thirty years before he was executed (Mark 6.14–29).

In his adult life, John received a call from God to be a prophet (Luke 3.2). He began to attract attention in the wilderness. People from all over Judea went to see him by the River Jordan. He called for national repentance, and many people crowded round him, many of whom he baptized in the River Jordan as they confessed their sins. The crowds talked about John's strange habits: he fed on locusts and wild honey; he was dressed in a robe made from camel's hair held together at the waist with a leather girdle. This vividly reminded the villagers of Judea of one of the great characters of their Bibles: Elijah, the greatest prophet of the Old Testament, of some nine hundred years before. Elijah had bravely pointed the people to their God. He was the model prophet, and when, centuries after Elijah lived, another prophet (Malachi, see Malachi 4.5) looked forward to the coming Day of the Lord when God himself would be revealed, he said that God would first of all send Elijah to prepare the way. Indeed, Luke's Gospel tells us that the angel had said to John's father before John was born: 'Many of the people of Israel will he bring back to the Lord their God. And he will go on before the Lord in the spirit and power of Elijah' (Luke 1.16–17).

So when John the Baptist appeared in the desert deliberately dressed like Elijah, the people knew that something was up. Something of momentous proportions was about to happen. Had not God promised to send Elijah to prepare for the coming of the Lord?

They listened with care to his words. He had baptized them with water, but One was to come who would baptize them with the Holy Spirit and with fire. John's Gospel describes John as 'sent from God' to 'bear witness to the light.' John bore witness that someone else was coming: the light of God which enlightens everyone was himself coming into the world.

And when John the Baptist sees Jesus coming towards him, he says 'This is he!'

We can picture a moment of immense drama. The crowds are around John near the River Jordan. Some, perhaps, have just been baptized. Many are calling on God for the forgiveness of their sins. All are looking forward expectantly to the coming of

God's Messiah. The anointed one of God has been promised for centuries. God would send a deliverer. God would himself in some way be present with them. God's kingly rule would be established. And John, in his strange Elijah clothes, is preparing them for this moment. The hot Judaean sun beats down on them. The cool river, running beside the riverside trees, seems to speak to them of freshness, of newness, of life. The sheep, perhaps with newborn lambs, are visible on the hillside, trying to find some shade. And now Jesus, who for some years has been working his way as a carpenter in the Nazareth family in which he had been brought up, walks towards John.

The Fourth Gospel tells us that John said: 'Look, the Lamb of God who takes away the sin of the world! This is the one I meant when I said "A man who comes after me has surpassed me because he was before me." I myself did not know him but the reason I came baptising with water was that he might be revealed to Israel' (John 1.29–31).

Jesus is God's coming One. Jesus is the expected Messiah. Jesus is the great prophet; the self-disclosure of God himself. It is to Jesus that all John's ministry and baptism have been pointers. And in the account given us by the Fourth Gospel, he is introduced by this strange phrase: Behold! the Lamb of God.

Why did John's Gospel record this particular title? Why did John the Baptist not simply say 'There is the Messiah'? or 'There is God's deliverer whom you have been seeking'? Why this unexpected phrase, 'the Lamb of God'? The following chapters of this book will, I hope, help us to answer this question. Each chapter concentrates on one picture, one lantern-slide, which we put into our projector, so that when the light shines through all of them, our composite picture describes 'the Lamb of God.'

The first of these slides is of the picture of the lamb which features in the story of Abraham and Isaac when they were together on Mount Moriah. The lamb in that story spoke of God's surprising provision at a time of uncertainty. Another slide tells the story of the Exodus, and the lamb there is the passover lamb of judgement and liberation. A third slide illustrates the sacrificial system described in the book of Leviticus, in which lambs were used in the burnt offering of consecration through which the worshippers discovered the logic and experience of forgiveness. A fourth picture comes from the Servant Songs of Isaiah, in which God's coming Messiah, the suffering servant, is portrayed as a lamb led to the slaughter. Alongside these lambs which symbolize provision, liberation, forgiveness and suffering, there is yet another picture which is drawn most clearly in the book of Enoch which is part of the Jewish Apocalyptic literature written between the time of our Old Testament and New Testament. The lamb there serves as a symbol of leadership, of conquest, of victory.

Perhaps, who knows?, some or all of these were in the minds of John the Baptist and his hearers, in the mind of the author of our Fourth Gospel, when one day near the River Jordan John pointed to Jesus and said 'Behold! the Lamb of God.'

The following chapters take one of these 'slides' each and explore how the stories painted on them contribute to our understanding of Jesus Christ as the

Lamb of God. They also explore some aspects of what living as Christians in the light of Jesus Christ might imply. By the end of the book, as we try to let the light of the Christian gospel shine through all of these pictures together, it is my hope and prayer that we will see more clearly the Lamb of God to which our Gospel records point.

Some Ideas for Using the Bible

Throughout these meditations, we will turn to some texts in the Bible. Some of my comments arise from my study of the texts. But other thoughts may come to you as you read: remember them, perhaps write them down. God has many different ways of teaching us through the pages of the Bible, and what you derive from reading the Bible is just as important as any comments I offer.

In a Bible study book of a generation ago, some suggestions were made for using the Bible as part of a personal time of devotion and prayer. They are suggestions that are well worth repeating. You may find that to use these suggestions opens up many things to say about the Bible text which I have not thought of. The older book was called *Search the Scriptures*[1], and this was its advice:

1. Open all such occasions [that is, for this sort of Bible study] with prayer for the Holy Spirit's light (Psalm 119.18). This is most important. The knowledge of what the Bible says, or even a correct understanding of its meaning, will not of itself bring spiritual life and power. 'What is needed,' says Andrew Murray, 'is very simple: the

determined refusal to attempt to deal with the written Word without the quickening Spirit. First, in a quiet act of worship, look to God to give and renew the workings of the Spirit within you; then, in a quiet act of faith, yield yourself to the power that dwells in you, and wait on Him, that not the mind alone, but the life in you, may be open to receive the Word.'

2. Ask to be guided to some definite thought for *yourself*.

3. Dwell prayerfully on this thought thus given – Is it a counsel, a precept, a warning, a promise, an experience, a command?

4. When its meaning is clear, use it as the basis of a prayer for grace to realize it in experience.

5. Yield the whole soul in full surrender to its truth and power.

6. Link it on to truths already known, and thereby strengthen the chain of experience.

7. Trust God to reproduce it in your life that day.

Jesus, Lamb of God, have mercy on us;
Jesus, Lamb of God, have mercy on us;
Jesus, Lamb of God, grant us your peace.

ONE

The Unexpected Lamb

In this chapter we use the story of Abraham and Isaac in Genesis 22, to think about God's unexpected grace, about the need to see our lives as part of a bigger picture and a greater truth, about the meaning of faith in times of uncertainty, about our prayers, and about the unfailing love of God.

We begin with a personal story.

A Child Died

I walked with them down the sloping path of the cemetery where they laid the small coffin to rest. The wind was blowing. The sun was shining. Just a hint of spring flowers coming into bud. Tears. Stillness. Silence. At the gathering afterwards, the feelings were more intense. Some were angry. How could God allow such a thing? If there were a God at all, he must be the devil. Or at least, not the all powerful, all-loving God in whom we had believed. Some were overcome with grief. For many, it seemed, the feelings were so intense that they seemed numbed by it all.

The death of a child is so hard to bear. A young adult knocked down in the street is tragic, but we are slowly coming to accept those headlines as one of the hazards of living in the twentieth century. A death in old age also brings its grief, but is something we all have to accept. But we are simply not ready or willing to accept the death of an apparently healthy, vital child. It turns all our expectations upside down. It faces us with questions we are not ready to ask, let alone have answers to. It contradicts what we thought we knew of God.

Christian people turn to God at a time like this, but God seems so contradictory. We want to pray, but do not know what to say. There seems such a mismatch between our usual pattern of prayers, and the reality we now face. The test of faith is to find a way of letting this experience be part of what we believe about the purpose and providence of God.

The New Testament offers us an example of this process in the way Jesus answered the disciples when they came to him asking for reasons (see John 9.1ff.). 'What went wrong with this blind man?' they asked. 'Was it his fault, or his parents, that he was born blind?' Jesus does not answer their question, but he does something else. He turns them around to face not back but forwards. 'It was not that this man sinned nor his parents, but that the works of God might be seen.' Jesus refuses to accept the question in terms of the past, in terms of 'why?'. He will only point forwards to God's future. He seems to be saying that the meaning of some of the contradictions and uncertainties will only be discerned in the glory of God that is yet to be seen. Our stories belong within a larger story that God is telling which, at present, we do not fully know.

A strange, and perhaps cruel way, we may think, to glorify God. The mourners at the cemetery thought so. It took time before they could pause and reflect on what our Lord was doing. He was taking up our needs, our uncertainties, our questions, and setting them within a bigger picture. This world, he reminds us, despite all appearances sometimes, is God's world. One day God's glory will be seen in all things. And the God whose glory will be seen is the God who makes himself known to us now as the God of faithful love. The God who enters into the sufferings and the questions and goes with us through them. And the only clue we are given to help us understand, is that suffering is the price we pay for love. It is because we love that we suffer. It is because God loves that he suffers.

In his profound little book, *Lament for a Son*[1], written to commemorate his son, a young man in his twenties killed in a climbing accident, Nicholas Wolterstorff, now professor of philosophy at Yale, explores his faith in God in the light of his deep sorrow. 'The tears of God,' he writes, 'are the meaning of history.'

This does not remove the hideous awfulness of an untimely death. It does, though, bring other light to shine on the puzzle and the perplexity, light which may yet give us strength to cope.

There is a children's hospice in Oxford. It is called Helen House after its first young member who spent her last days there in the care of nuns at the convent in whose grounds the hospice was built. It provides a place of support for parents whose children are terminally ill as well as a caring family for the young people themselves for the last weeks of their lives. At a service of remembrance there, the then Archbishop of Canterbury, Robert Runcie, included these words in his sermon: 'Too often there is talk of lives cut short, as if length of years is what life is really about. But there is a greater truth: that no life, however short, is ever wasted; that no life in which love has been given and received is anything other than complete.'

'There is a greater truth.' We are invited to set ourselves and our sorrows and questions in the context of the providence of a God who loves and suffers and weeps and gives. And sometimes in that process, the one whom Gerard Hughes aptly called 'the God of Surprises'[2] opens up to us resources of unexpected grace.

Abraham and Isaac

There was a strange providence at work on the day the Lord tested Abraham. The story is told in Genesis 22. 'Take your son, your only son Isaac, whom you love, and go to the region of Moriah. Sacrifice him there as a burnt offering' (Genesis 22.2).

Here is the whole narrative:

Some time later God tested Abraham. He said to him, 'Abraham!' 'Here I am,' he replied. Then God said, 'Take your son, your only son Isaac, whom you love, and go to the region of Moriah. Sacrifice him there as a burnt offering on one of the mountains I will tell you about.'

Early the next morning Abraham got up and saddled his donkey. He took with him two of his servants and his son Isaac. Whe he had cut enough wood for the burnt offering, he set out for the place God had told him about. On the third day Abraham looked up and saw the place in the distance. He said to his servants, 'Stay here with the donkey while I and the boy go over there. We will worship and then we will come back to you.'

Abraham took the wood for the burnt offering and placed it on his son Isaac, and he himself carried the fire and the knife. As the two of them went on together, Isaac spoke up and said to his father Abraham, 'Father?' 'Yes, my son?' Abraham replied. 'The fire and the wood are here,' Isaac said, 'but where is the lamb for the burnt offering?' Abraham answered, 'God himself will provide the lamb for the burnt offering, my son.' And the two of them went on together.

When they reached the place God had told him about, Abraham built an altar there and arranged the wood on it. He bound his son Isaac and laid him on the altar, on top of the wood. Then he reached out his hand and took the knife to slay his son. But the angel of the Lord called out to him from heaven, 'Abraham! Abraham!'

'Here I am,' he replied. 'Do not lay a hand on the boy,' he said. 'Do not do anything to him. Now I know that you fear God, because you have not withheld from me your son, your only son.'

Abraham looked up and there in a thicket he saw a ram caught by its horns. He went over and took the ram and sacrificed it as a burnt offering instead of his son. So Abraham called that place 'The Lord will Provide'.

Abraham had been tested before. According to the Genesis story, he had endured many harassments and trials. He had been driven out of his home by famine. He had twice been separated from his wife. He had parted from his nephew, and had saved this nephew at peril of his own life. But this new test was of a different order. This test was the loss of his son.

Clearly for us all the moral horror of child sacrifice – an ultimately appalling form of child abuse – and the intense anguish the boy's mother must have felt, as well as Abraham's own feelings, crowd in on us as we read the story. We cannot bear the immorality of it all. It is not easily put alongside our image of the God of love. We may be reassured by those scholars who see this story as a response by a writer of Israel arguing against Canaanite child sacrifice. But for most of us, the story raises at least as many moral problems as it solves. There is a proper place for a full discussion of these problems. But for our purposes of exploring the place of the lamb in the story, we must not let these proper concerns get in the way trying to make sense of the text as it stands. We need to find ourselves caught up into the story, which is presented as a test of faith, given to Abraham by God.

The test concerns the loss of Abraham's son, his only son whom he loved. This son embodied all Abraham's future, or rather, God's promise of a future. And not Abraham's only, for the future of the whole people of God was involved. In a sense, the whole salvation of the world was bound up with this son. For had not God promised Abraham: 'You will be the father of many nations' (Genesis 17.4)? 'You must keep my covenant, you and your descendants after you' (Genesis 17.9). All the promises of God are bound up in Isaac, Abraham's only son, a divine gift to Abraham and Sarah in their old age.

And the test is that God now commands Abraham to make the supreme sacrifice: to offer his son as a sacrifice.

At the start of the Abraham story in Genesis 12, he is asked to leave aside all his past, and step out in faith in the God who called him. Now he is being asked to set aside all his future as well.

But it is worse even than this, for Abraham is depicted as not merely faced with a conflict of interests. All too often in this world, moral conflict comes to us as a clash of values or principles, and we may be forced to choose between lesser evils or greater goods. But Abraham's test was more profound. Not for him merely a conflict of principles; not simply a divided conscience. But a conflict in the very nature of God. Abraham experiences the ultimate paradox, the ultimate absurdity. There is a stark contradiction between God's promise in the past: 'I will give you a son' (Genesis 17.15ff.), and his command in the present: 'Take your son and sacrifice him' (Genesis 22.2).

What is God up to? How does this world make sense? How can we trust a God who seems to contradict himself? What are we to do when God seems to take on a double character?

Although we, the readers, know that God's command to sacrifice Isaac is a test, and that there is a hint right from the beginning of the story (Genesis 22.1) that God knows what is going on, Abraham does not know this. Abraham is sent out on the most radical test of obedience. He had to obey the command and trust the promise, though for all his experience, he could not see how the two fitted together.

A Hint of Hope?

But this is the point at which his faith shines
through. Centuries later the writer of the letter to
the Hebrews reflected on this:

> By faith Abraham, when God tested him, offered
> Isaac as a sacrifice. He who had received the
> promises was about to sacrifice his one and only
> son, even though God had said to him, 'It is
> through Isaac that your offspring will be reck-
> oned.' Abraham reasoned that God could raise the
> dead, and figuratively speaking, he did receive
> Isaac back from death (Hebrews 11.17ff.).

Is there a hint of this hope in the story itself? He has
set off with Isaac and some travelling companions to
Mount Moriah. On the third day they see their des-
tination. Abraham and Isaac leave the other two, and
Abraham says 'Stay here with the donkey while I
and the boy go over there. We will worship and
then we will come back to you' (Genesis 22.5). The
plain reading of the text is that Abraham expected to
come back with Isaac. But how could this be if Isaac
was to be offered as a sacrifice? Only if Isaac was
raised from the dead! Here then, says the author of
Hebrews, is a 'figure' – a 'prefiguring' – of resurrection (Hebrews 11.19). Perhaps it is this faith that is
also hinted at in the Fourth Gospel, where Jesus says
'Your father Abraham rejoiced at the thought of
seeing my day' (John 8.56).

So how is this apparent contradiction in God
resolved? How does faith triumph in the face of
paradox and uncertainty? How can death become life?

We notice Abraham's 'self-abandonment to divine providence'[3]: 'Here I am.' We notice how his trust in God has to be weighed against all common sense, against his human affection, and against his lifelong ambition. He simply took the risk. Rather as Ransom, using New Testament language, in C. S. Lewis' *Voyage to Venus*[4] confronts a fearful uncertainty before him on the planet Perelandra with the words 'In the name of the Father, and of the Son, and of the Holy Ghost, here goes...'

And at this point, the story talks about a lamb.

The Lamb

Abraham took the wood for the burnt offering and placed it on his son Isaac, and he himself carried the fire and the knife. As the two of them went on together, Isaac spoke up and said to his father Abraham, 'Father?' 'Yes, my son?' Abraham replied. 'The fire and the wood are here,' Isaac said, 'but where is the lamb for the burnt offering?' Abraham answered, 'God himself will provide the lamb for the burnt offering, my son.' And the two of them went on together.

What, then, is the function of the lamb in this story?

Abraham's sure trust in the lamb that God would provide is his way of saying that when things seem hopeless, all means fail, all ways ahead seem closed, and yet God has called us, then we must trust in the providence and provision of God. God will open a way where there is none. Faith is what God gives us to help us hold on to God even in the place of extremity and uncertainty. Faith affirms: 'God will provide.' Not necessarily as we expect, but 'that the work of God might be displayed' (John 9.3).

The rest of the story of Abraham and Isaac is told with great tension. Every action is described. Abraham builds an altar, lays the wood in order, binds Isaac his son, lays him on the altar, puts forth his hand, takes a knife . . .

And then, from the place of death, God speaks a word of life. The angel calls Abraham's name. The lamb of Abraham's hopes becomes the ram caught in a thicket by its horns. The ram is substituted in the place of Isaac. The ram dies in his place, and Isaac is called back to life and rises up from the altar of death.

So the lamb stands for God's provision, for God's gracious gift. In the place of uncertainty and pain and questions, in place of paradox where to trust seems absurd and all we have to go on is a confusing word from God, there God provides. The lamb does not resolve the paradox, but becomes in a sense part of the paradox in such a way that Abraham can now go on with his life in the faith that, despite all Abraham's perplexity, God has never let go of his hand.

The lamb also stands for the fact that God works through the ordinary things. To take a 'ram's eye view' of this story, this was no special ram, just one among many roaming the hills that morning. And yet God took one of the ordinary, everyday features of that day as a 'means of grace' for Abraham.

Life Laid Down: Life Restored

The lamb also vividly illustrates that central biblical theme that life laid down becomes the means of life restored. Despite all our dislike of the language of sacrifice, sacrifice is in fact a principle of life throughout the universe. We see this in the world of nature. The leaves fall from the trees and rot in the ground, to provide nourishment for next year's growth. The seed dies so that the primroses can bring us a glimpse that spring is on its way. All carnivorous animals eat the flesh of other animals as part of their food-chain. The New Testament uses this imagery when it speaks of a corn of wheat falling into the ground and dying, so that there may be much fruit (John 12.24). St Paul makes a great deal of the imagery of seeds dying so that there can be new life, in his magisterial chapter on resurrection in his first letter to the Corinthians[5]. The cycle of life-giving and death so that other life may grow is part of the evolutionary story. It is also part of the story of moral development. For in human moral terms also, life given and shared is always part of the creative process of making life new. We could think of grand examples, such as the self-sacrifice of 'Titus' Oates who walked out of Captain Scott's tent into the Antarctic blizzard in the hope of saving the lives of his companions. And of Jesus' own statement: 'Greater love has no-one than this, that one lay down his life for his friends' (John 15.13). But it happens in much more ordinary and everyday ways as well. Whenever a parent puts the needs of her child above her own desires; whenever a husband or wife puts the well-being of the spouse before their own; whenever a child shares her sweets with a friend, there is a measure of sacrifice for the sake of the other, and life is thereby enriched. And here in the Abraham story, God the provider, God the life-giver, acts through costly life-giving grace.

And the lamb tells us one thing more: for from the very beginning God knew what he was doing. Here another story is being told – a 'greater truth' – and Abraham's story is being caught up into it. Although for a long and painful time God kept Abraham in the dark, here at the end of the story, Abraham comes to see what before he could only hope for: the reality of God's care and provision. God's command has been obeyed; God's promise has been fulfilled.

In his secret providence, God asks his servant to walk the dark and dangerous road of trusting faith, looking to God's future in hope. Eventually, God stretches out his hand in visible tokens of loving grace. Here is the unexpectedness of God; here is God's surprise.

Providence and Prayer

There are two particular themes we can take further from this in terms of Christian discipleship, and the first is the relationship of this understanding of providence to the life of prayer.

As Peter Forster once put it: 'What a man believes or does not believe about prayer is a good guide to his religious beliefs in general ... more particularly, what a man does about prayer is an indication of what he believes about it.'[6] In Abraham we see a faithful response to God's providence, despite all his uncertainties. That response is very close to what I mean by prayer. To quote what I wrote elsewhere:

Prayer is, as it were, the flip side to the doctrine of providence. Prayer is the acknowledgement, not of the psychological benefit of some mythological exercise, but of the fact that we *believe* that God is there, God cares, God rules and God provides, and believe it in such a way that we are ready to do something on that basis, namely speak to him. Providence reminds us of our creatureliness and dependence on God, and that together with all people, we stand under God's lordship; prayer is an activity by which we acknowledge that we cannot be our own lord.

Providence reminds us that everything is not ultimately absurd or meaningless; prayer is our way of expressing our 'yes' to the conviction that God is working his purposes out in nature, in human beings, in history. Providence is a reminder that the Lord is a God of grace and generosity; prayer is our way of responding to his invitation to be a member of his covenant family, his son or daughter, his co-worker in this world. Providence reminds us that the living God is not an irresistible fate before whom we can only keep silent and passive; prayer is our response to God's invitation to share fellowship with him, an expression of our union with him. ... By prayer, therefore, we both express our trust in God's providence, and discover how our own wills are to be more aligned with his sovereign and loving will for us. Our action in prayer is met by his transforming answer.'[7]

Life through death

The second theme on which we can elaborate briefly
is the way the Abraham story gives a message of life
through struggle and death. The cross of Jesus Christ
is the central heart of Christian discipleship; his death
and resurrection are the very heart of our faith. But
the task of trying to put into words the meaning of
his death has been one with which theologians have
struggled throughout the centuries. There have been
a number of so-called 'theories of the atonement'.
We shall notice some of these throughout this book.
Among them are the 'ransom' theory associated with
some of the theologians of the early church; and the
'satisfaction' theory of some medieval scholars such as
Anselm. The Reformers, such as Calvin, spoke of the
cross in terms of 'substitutionary atonement'. Abelard
in the Middle Ages and Hastings Rashdall at the turn
of this century both developed 'theories' of the
atonement in terms of the moral influence of Jesus'
self-giving love. Yet others (Luther and Gustav
Aulén, for example), speak of the cross in terms of
Christ's victory over evil. As we shall see, there are
aspects of all of these theories of atonement hinted at
in the various images of 'the Lamb of God'.

There is, however, one other New Testament
image which is perhaps more easily linked to the
lamb in the story of Abraham and Isaac than some of
the others. This is an image picked up in Frances
Young's book *Can These Dry Bones Live?*[8] Professor
Young turns back to an image used by St Paul in
Romans 8: that of the labour pains before a birth.

This is what St Paul says:

I consider that our present sufferings are not worth

comparing with the glory that will be revealed in us. The creation waits in eager expectation for the sons of God to be revealed. ... We know that the whole creation has been groaning as in the pain of childbirth right up the present time. Not only so, but we ourselves, who have the first fruits of the Spirit, groan inwardly as we wait eagerly for our adoption as sons, the redemption of our bodies. (Romans 8.18ff.)

Professor Young had argued that 'the meaning of the cross must be related in some way not just to sin, but to all suffering, all pain, all disaster, all injustice, all decay and death – indeed to all that is wrong with the creation, human nature and human society as we know it.' And then she develops her moving discussion of atonement by starting with Paul's words in Romans 8 about the redemption of the whole creation which has been groaning in travail. There are many biblical references to labour and childbirth which refer to God. Sometimes they are used to refer to the suffering of the world as in a sense part of God's 'labour to bring forth a new people, restoration, new life, new hope'.[9] This is surely part of St Paul's imagery in Romans 8, where he speaks of the whole creation groaning, waiting for redemption. The link between suffering and the gift of new life, even in the place of death, which we see in the lamb on Mount Moriah, is a link which St Paul then goes on to make in his reference to Jesus as a gift of God's love.

The supreme visible token of God's love is the gift of his own Son, as they walk the way of the cross, 'both of them together'. And 'he who did not spare his own Son, but gave him up for us all – will he

not also, along with him, graciously give us all
things?' (Romans 8.32). So who, cries St Paul, can
separate us from God's love?

At the end of the day, that was all the grieving
parents of the little child could hold on to. Through
their tears, they learned of the tears of God. Through
their puzzlement in the darkness of unknowing, they
learned that God was holding their hand. Through
the unexpectedness of grace, God provided them
with grace to go on.

May God help us hold on to the God who provides, the Lord who – despite all appearances some-
time – holds us with a love that will not let us go.

* * *

For Further Reflection:

What, then, shall we say in response to this? If
God is for us, who can be against us? He who did
not spare his own Son but gave him up for us all
– will he not also, along with him, graciously give
us all things?... Who shall separate us from the
love of Christ? Shall trouble or hardship or persecution or famine or nakedness or danger or
sword?... No, in all these things we are more
than conquerors through him who loved us. For I
am convinced that neither death nor life, neither
angels nor demons, neither the present nor the
future, nor any powers, neither height nor depth,
nor anything else in all creation, will be able to
separate us from the love of God that is in Christ
Jesus our Lord' (taken from Romans 8.31–39).

* * *

SOME QUESTIONS

1. Can you think of any times when God has

seemed very far away? Are there any ways in which we can understand those times as part of a 'greater truth' about God and his purposes?

2. Does it help to think of prayer as lining our wills up with God's will?

3. When has the 'God of Surprises' especially reminded us of his love? There may be particular personal moments we can think of.

* * *

O Love that wilt not let me go,
I rest my weary soul in Thee:
I give Thee back the life I owe,
That in Thine ocean depths its flow
May richer, fuller be.

O Light that followest all my way,
I yield my flickering torch to Thee:
My heart restores its borrowed ray,
That in Thy sunshine's blaze its day
May brighter, fairer be.

O Joy that seekest me through pain,
I cannot close my heart to Thee:
I trace the rainbow through the rain,
And feel the promise is not vain,
That morn shall tearless be.

O Cross that liftest up my head,
I dare not ask to fly from Thee:
I lay in dust life's glory dead,
And from the ground there blossoms red
Life that shall endless be.

George Matheson (1842–1906)

TWO

The Liberation Lamb

Our second theme, the second slide to place in our projector, is a picture of liberation. The lamb in this chapter is the passover lamb at the centre of the story of the Exodus. We will think about the way the story of the Exodus, as told in Exodus 12, became such a pivotal event in the minds of God's people in the Old Testament, and what liberation is for, as well as what it is from. We begin with some reflections on the theme of liberation. 'Liberation' is a cry that spans the centuries.

Freedom!

After too many long days, months, years as a hostage in Beirut, the day came when Terry Waite was to be released. The tabloid headline in large letters over his photograph simply said 'FREEDOM'. The shackles had been unlocked, the darkness had lifted, the solitariness was at an end. To come were the hard months of readjustment, of living again the free life.

Freedom is one of our most precious values. Richard Attenborough's film *Cry Freedom* is a poignant exploration of the significance of the life and death of black South African Stephen Biko. Biko's had been the Bantu voice of black consciousness in the 1970s. His quiet leadership had been threatening to the white authorities. He was impri-

soned and died in police custody. Biko's was one
voice crying for freedom for black people from the
injustices and oppression of apartheid. When apartheid was finally dismantled in spring 1993, one word
on Archbishop Desmond Tutu's lips was 'freedom'.
Now the peoples of South Africa are engaged in the
long and no doubt precarious process of discovering
what the life of freedom from apartheid means in
practice. For the State President, Nelson Mandela,
freedom has involved going back to the place where
for more than two decades he was imprisoned
because of his political quest for the freedom his
people are now beginning to realize.

The cry for freedom is worldwide. Wherever
people feel themselves to be oppressed and held in
bondage, people long to be free. Recent decades
have seen various 'liberation' crusades, such as
women's liberation and gay liberation. Much of the
impetus of what has come to be known as liberation
theology, as this has developed in Latin America, is
a cry for freedom from social and political oppression, and a way of interpreting the gospel of Jesus
Christ as a means of finding such liberty. One of
the guiding theological themes of liberation theology is the story of the Exodus: the time in the consciousness of the people of God in the Old
Testament when they were set free after years of
being slaves in Egypt. This story came to its climax
on passover night, when God sets his people free.
This story will be the major theme of this chapter,
and at its centre is the passover lamb. But before we
come to look at it in more detail, we need to
explore a little more fully what we mean by
'freedom'.

Personal Freedoms

Freedom is not only a political and social word; it can have a strong personal dimension also. Individual people can be held in bondage and long for liberty. And the chains do not have to be made of metal. There can be chains of memories of past hurts which still hold a person in their grip. Numbers of people are coming to terms with the emotional bondage of having been abused – emotionally, physically, sexually – as children. Some of these people are discovering, through therapy or other ministries of healing, that it is possible to find freedom from some of these scars. It often needs specialist help. It takes time. It is a hard, long struggle. But there can be a measure of liberty.

There can be chains of habits which have developed over a long period of time, and from which a person cannot now escape. Some of these are emotional habits learned when we were young, patterns of response to people and situations which we would like to be different. Some of these might be habits of thought: we constantly find ourselves running in the same grooves, and some of the beliefs we carried round with us are actually enslaving. Albert Ellis is one clinical psychologist who has identified a number of common ideas which he calls irrational, but which many of us constantly carry in our heads.

For example, if I am constantly saying to myself things like: 'I must be approved of by every other significant person in my life; I must be thoroughly competent, adequate and achieving in everything; when people act unfairly, I should blame them, damn them, see them as bad ...' and so on, I am asking to feel bad about myself. These can be destructive mental chains, leading, often, to anxiety or depression. It is not always the case, because our emotions are very complex parts of us, but it is sometimes true that what we believe in our heads will affect how we feel in our hearts.

If I believe that I am only worthwhile as a person if I get very high marks for all my examination papers, then when I do not do too well I will inevitably feel a failure, a disaster, a no-good person. The equation 'worth because of achievement' is one that many of us carry round with us, and it has a built-in disappointment. If we are able to learn to think differently about ourselves, to change those habits of thought which are holding us in their trap, there can be liberty. Sometimes this is best done with help from someone else – and it takes time to change habits which we have developed over many years. But change is possible.

There can be fears and phobias which restrict us and hold us in their thrall. Some people live in constant fear of one thing or another. Many counsellors and therapists are skilled at helping people live with less fear. This can involve discovering the truth which the New Testament expresses in this way: love casts out fear (1 John 4.18).

Freedom within Limits

Clearly, there are limits to freedoms. Human beings are not free to fly through the air like a swallow, nor live under water like a fish. There are physical and environmental limits to our freedoms. And yet those very limits also enable freedoms of other sorts.

Because of our physical make-up, we are free to do things which birds and fish cannot do. There are other limits also, social constraints which restrict certain patterns of behaviour but enable others. Every society has some regulation for sexual behaviour, for example (whether it is kept to or not). This is (negatively) to protect vulnerable people from being exploited, and to contain and channel strong passions so that they are not inappropriately expressed. But also (positively) this enables the free and joyous celebration of love and its passions within an appropriate creative context.

So there are certain moral boundaries within which there is a freedom for life and for living, but beyond which we can find ourselves trapped by guilt, social disapproval or a heavy conscience. Societies have developed moral codes to guide peoples' behaviour in ways which enable people to live freely within limits, but which do not unjustly infringe the freedoms of other people.

Some of us are afraid of freedom. As Erich Fromm has argued, there is a 'fear of freedom',[1] which keeps many of us tied to our shackles, but at least there we know where we are: the outside world is just too frightening to face.

We need, therefore, not only to ask 'freedom from what?' but also 'freedom for what?' If we are set free from certain constraints which have hindered us and held us down, we can then ask 'Can I face my new freedom?' and 'how am I to use my new freedom – what is it for?'

Both these questions – freedom from? and freedom for? – were appropriate to the people of God whose story is written in the book of Exodus.

Passover Night

For several hundred years the people of Israel had
been slaves, treated cruelly, and used as a task force
for the various building programmes of their Egyptian masters. They had cried to the Lord for their
liberty. They had reminded him of his calling them
to be a people of his own. In fact, when the Lord
told Moses to negotiate with Pharaoh for the Israelites' release, the Lord had spoken most tenderly of
his covenant people: 'Israel is my firstborn' (Exodus
4.22).

The time came when, we read, God remembered
the covenant promises that he made to Abraham,
Isaac and Jacob so long before. God called to Moses
at the burning bush and made himself known as
Yahweh, the Lord. He told Moses his name: 'I AM
WHO I AM.' Yahweh gave Moses a commission to
lead God's people to freedom from the domination
of Pharaoh.

After several attempts at negotiations, and a series
of plagues and disasters sent by the Lord upon
Egypt, eventually the night of release arrived. It is
forever remembered in the consciousness of the
people of God as the night of passover. And its
central feature is a lamb.

The story is told in Exodus 12.

The Lord said to Moses and Aaron in Egypt, 'This
month is to be for you the first month, the first
month of your year. Tell the whole community of
Israel that on the tenth day of this month each
man is to take a lamb for his family, one for each
household. If any household is too small for a

whole lamb, they must share one with their nearest neighbour, having taken into account the number of people there are. You are to determine the amount of lamb needed in accordance with what each person will eat. The animals you choose must be year-old males without defect, and you may take them from the sheep or the goats. Take care of them until the fourteenth day of the month, when all the people of the community of Israel must slaughter them at twilight. Then they are to take some of the blood and put it on the sides and tops of the door-frames of the houses where they eat the lambs. That same night they are to eat the meat roasted over the fire, along with bitter herbs, and bread made without yeast. Do not eat the meat raw or cooked in water, but roast it over the fire – head, legs and inner parts. Do not leave any of it till morning; if some is left till morning, you must burn it. This is how you are to eat it: with your cloak tucked into your belt, your sandals on your feet and your staff in your hand. Eat it in haste; it is the Lord's Passover.

On that same night I will pass through Egypt and strike down every firstborn – both men and animals – and I will bring judgment on all the gods of Egypt; I am the Lord. The blood will be a sign for you on the houses where you are; and when I see the blood, I will pass over you. No destructive plague will touch you when I strike Egypt. . . .'

At midnight the Lord struck down all the firstborn in Egypt, from the firstborn of Pharaoh, who sat on the throne, to the firstborn of the prisoner, who was in the dungeon, and the firstborn of all the livestock as well. Pharaoh and all his officials and all the Egyptians got up during the night, and there was loud wailing in Egypt, for there was not a house without someone dead.

During the night Pharaoh summoned Moses and Aaron and said, 'Up! Leave my people, you and the Israelites! Go, worship the Lord as you have requested. Take your flocks and herds, as you have said, and go. And also bless me.' (Exodus 12.1–13; 29–32)

Let us now unpack some of the detail of this narrative. First of all, the Lord instructs Moses to tell all the congregation to prepare a lamb: one lamb for each household. The provision is quite specific:

Tell the whole community of Israel that on the tenth day of this month each man is to take a lamb for his family, one for each household. If any household is too small for a whole lamb, they must share one with their nearest neighbour, having taken into account the number of people there are. You are to determine the amount of lamb needed in accordance with what each person will eat.

In other words, the lamb was to be chosen according to the needs of the people. It was not to be too big; indeed if after eating the roasted lamb any was left over, it was to be burned. The lamb was chosen to fit the peoples' needs.

Second, the lamb had to be pure: 'The animals you choose must be year-old males without defect.'

Third, the people were told to kill the lamb, 'Then they are to take some of the blood and put it on the sides and tops of the door-frames of the houses where they eat the lambs.' What was the purpose of this?

The explanation is given by the Lord to Moses. The Lord will pass through the land of Egypt that night: 'I will pass through Egypt and strike down every firstborn – both men and animals – and I will bring judgment on all the gods of Egypt; I am the Lord.'

'Egypt' and 'Pharaoh', the ruler of Egypt, have become symbols for slavery, bondage, loss of liberty, oppression. We recall that God had earlier told Moses to say to Pharaoh that Israel is God's firstborn: 'I told you, "Let my son go, so that he may worship me." But you refused to let him go; so I will kill your firstborn son' (Exodus 4.23). What has been described (by Alec Motyer) as the 'contest of the firstborns' is clearly understood here as symbolic of a deeper contest: between Yahweh, the Lord God of Israel, and the gods of the Egyptians. Behind the slave-driving taskmasters of Egypt lies the domination of the Egyptian gods. God's own people, his firstborn, must be set free; if Pharaoh will not let them go, his own firstborn will die as a sign of divine judgement.

Judgement and Mercy

So on passover night, the Lord is passing through the land of Egypt in judgement. The firstborn of Egypt – the symbol of their continuing life – will perish. The firstborn in each family will die as a sign of God's judgement against the evil gods of Egypt. But in this judgement, God also had a purpose of mercy and liberation. For passover night is not only the night of the death of the firstborn of Egypt, it is the night of the release of the first-born of God.

And it is in this linking of judgement and death with mercy and liberty that the significance of the lamb in the story becomes clearer: 'The blood [of the lamb] will be a sign for you on the houses where you are; and when I see the blood, I will pass over you. No destructive plague will touch you when I strike Egypt.'

There could be no clearer indication that the lamb dies in the place of the firstborn of Israel than the statement later in the chapter after the Lord of judgement has swept through the land: 'There was not a house without someone dead' (Exodus 12.30). In each *Egyptian* household, there lies dead the firstborn son 'from the firstborn of Pharaoh who sat on the throne, to the firstborn of the prisoner, who was in the dungeon, and the firstborn of all the livestock as well'. In each *Israelite* household there lay dead the lamb of sacrifice.

For God's firstborn son, the people of Israel, there was safety from the judgement of God found by sheltering in the place that was marked by the blood of the lamb. The lamb died in the place of the people, its blood a sign of the coming together of God's judgement and God's mercy. The same action which brought judgement on the land of Egypt also secured the release of God's people from slavery.

Passover night is the bringing together of judgement and mercy, and through that action, there is liberty.

Pharaoh's reaction to this night was dramatic. He summoned Moses and Aaron and said: 'Up! Leave my people, you and the Israelites! Go, worship the Lord as you have requested. Take your flocks and herds, as you have said, and go. And also bless me.' So the people of Israel were set free from their slavery. They were free to go. But it was also clear to them what their freedom was *for*. They were set free to serve the Lord. Their freedom was a freedom for a new sort of service. The people were told, in fact, to eat the passover lamb in a specific way: 'This is how you are to eat it: with your cloak tucked into your belt, your sandals on your feet and your staff in your hand. Eat it in haste; it is the Lord's Passover.'

They were to be ready for action, ready to move, ready for change.

Passover night was not a night of release for the life of luxury and leisure. It was the beginning of a journey, a pilgrimage, an adventure of faith, a new opportunity for service for the living God. In fact, as it turned out, there was a desert to be negotiated and many battles to be fought.

The Exodus as a Symbol for Liberation

It is not surprising that the Exodus story has had such a powerful influence on liberation movements. With its powerful political themes of justice seen in judgement and mercy, and the release of those oppressed, the Exodus has motivated believers to seek to express in contemporary social and political life some of the implications of what we may call the

passover gospel. The Exodus story has become a sort
of symbol for political and social liberation. There is
strong evidence of the use of the story in this way in
the Old Testament. Very soon after the account of
the passover night in the book of Exodus itself, for
example, the newly freed people are taken to Mount
Sinai where Moses receives the Ten Commandments
from God. As Exodus 20 makes clear, these commandments are specifically set in the context of
exodus: 'I am the Lord your God who brought you
out of Egypt, out of the land of slavery ...' Now,
therefore, you should live like this: with no other
gods, no graven images, respecting the honour of
Yahweh's name, and Yahweh's sabbath – in other
words, loving God with heart and soul and mind
and strength. Honour parental authority and show
your neighbours respect for the right to life, to
marital fidelity, to their own property, to an honest
reputation – in other words, love your neighbour
enough not to covet.

It has been suggested that these commandments
may well have formed the basis for ancient Israel's
criminal law. It seems very likely that many of the
detailed regulations for agricultural, matrimonial,
economic and religious life were related to these
commandments. Society was intended to reflect
something of the character of Yahweh which is
depicted in the Ten Commandments, the God 'who
brought you out of Egypt to be your God' (Leviticus 22.32). When, later, the Deuteronomist was
exploring some of the significance of these commandments (Deuteronomy 6.4ff.), it is made clear
that the Exodus tradition is to be carried on in the
teaching of the next generation:

In the future, when your son asks you, 'What is
the meaning of the stipulations, decrees and laws
the Lord our God has commanded you?' tell him:
'We were slaves of Pharaoh's in Egypt, but the
Lord brought us out of Egypt with a mighty hand
... to bring us in and give us the land that he promised on oath to our forefathers.' (Deuteronomy
6.20ff.)

Remember that you were slaves in Egypt and
the Lord your God redeemed you. That is why I
give you this command today' (Deuteronomy
15.15).

On the Side of the Powerless

There was, however, more to it than that. The
Exodus story was also used as a motivation for a specific and special concern for the disadvantaged, the
poor, the alien, the widow. 'Do not oppress an alien;
you yourselves know how it feels to be aliens,
because you were aliens in Egypt' (Exodus 23.9). Or
again, 'The Lord your God ... shows no partiality
and accepts no bribes. He defends the cause of the
fatherless and the widow, and loves the alien, giving
him food and clothing. And you are to love those
who are aliens, for you yourselves were aliens in
Egypt' (Deuteronomy 10.17ff.). Or again,

Do not deprive the alien or the fatherless of
justice, or take the cloak of the widow as a pledge.
Remember that you were slaves in Egypt and the
Lord your God redeemed you from there. That is
why I command you to do this' (Deuteronomy
24.17).

The same theme continues in many of the major prophets of generations later.[2] The social life of the people is intended to demonstrate the justice and mercy of the God who redeemed them from Egypt and set them free to serve him in holiness and right-eousness, especially on behalf of the poor, the pow-erless, the marginalized and disadvantaged. The great twentieth-century Swiss theologian, Karl Barth, expressed it powerfully in these words:

> The human righteousness required by God and established in obedience, the righteousness which, according to Amos 5.24 should pour down as a mighty stream – has necessarily the character of a vindication of right in favour of the threatened innocent, the oppressed poor, widows, orphans and aliens. For this reason, in the relations and events in the life of His people, God always takes His stand unconditionally and passionately on this side, and on this side alone: against the lofty and on behalf of the lowly; against those who already enjoy right and privilege, and on behalf of those who are denied and deprived of it.[3]

Social and political freedoms are part of the Exodus, part of the passover gospel.

Christ, the Passover Lamb

It is not surprising that the New Testament picks up this Exodus theme in more than one place. One very clear reference focuses more on a personal than a social liberty. In Paul's first letter to the Corinthians, he specifically links Jesus Christ to the passover: 'Christ, our Passover lamb, has been sacrificed. Therefore let us keep the Festival, not with the old yeast, the yeast of malice and wickedness, but with bread without yeast, the bread of sincerity and truth' (1 Corinthians 5.7).

St Paul is here dealing less with social justice than with the problem of a specific and tolerated sin within the community: a man living with his father's wife. Such irregular sexual relationships should not be tolerated. The Corinthians' boasting of their spiritual health should be carefully checked in the light of such excesses in their community. The new life of Christian discipleship involves a cleansing out of the old patterns of slavery to sin, and a pilgrimage in the light of the truth of Christ which sets free. How can they be falling back into such sinful ways? The passover lamb has been sacrificed! They should be celebrating their freedom from such sins by walking out in sincerity and truth.

Christ sets free – free from the slavery of sinful habits (though we all know that often takes hard work, time, and the gradual growing of the new habits of repentance and faith in God's grace); free for walking with Christ in what St Paul often calls 'the new life'.

But it is not only freedom from the gross and obvious sins such as are described as happening at Corinth that Christ sets free. There are the hidden secret sins of our hearts we would be ashamed to share. They can hold us in a slavery as strong as any outward immorality. We are invited to see Christ as the Lamb of God who takes away the sins of the world, one in whose death we can find the liberty of a new power to live differently. And there are other freedoms, too.

Free to Be Ourselves

Some of us need to hear again the freedom from the 'condemnation of law'. Some Christians are prone to hear the voice of God as a threatening moral demand. Outside the grace of Christ, God's moral character does show up our distance from God, and the New Testament does speak of the law of God in terms of condemnation. But the gospel of grace is that in Christ we are set free from this condemning sense of law: 'There is now no condemnation' (Romans 8.1). We can be set free to be instead 'under Christ's law' (1 Corinthians 9.21).

Some of us need to realize a proper freedom from the burden of other peoples' expectancies and others' criticisms. The gospel can liberate us from being burdened by the critical judgement of other people. Paul himself guarded against the hostile criticism of other Christians. He wrote, 'I care very little if I am judged by you or by any human court; indeed, I do not even judge myself. My conscience is clear, but that does not make me innocent. It is the Lord who judges me' (1 Corinthians 4.3). On the other hand, Paul took seriously the needs and concerns of others, and placed an importance on a clear conscience. Nevertheless what mattered most was God's view of him as someone set free to serve Christ.

Free to Differ

Then there needs to be a freedom to disagree about

things which do not matter *that* much. Christians of
an earlier age used to speak about 'things indifferent'
– ways of Christian living and behaving on which it
was perfectly all right for different people to take
different views. We must agree on the 'fundamentals'
of the gospel, they said, but there are many issues on
which the Bible does not speak, on which Christian
tradition is not clear, and on which it is legitimate to
hold differing views.

The history of the Christian Church has many
examples of questions on which Christians have
come to different conclusions, or in their own consciences have chosen to act in ways different from
that which other Christians believe to be right. Some
might be very serious. On issues of justice and peace,
for example, in situations of international conflict.
For several centuries in the early Church, Christians
were mostly pacifist, for political and theological
reasons. By the time of Augustine, when the Roman
Empire had officially become Christian, there were
theologians who – in order to vindicate God's justice
in the face of the threat of evil barbarian invaders –
argued that a Christian may bear arms in war. Both
the 'just war' tradition, and several pacifist traditions,
have existed in the church, both in their different
ways trying to bear witness to God's justice and
God's call for peacemakers.

Another more personal question is the permissi-
bility of divorce. On the whole the Catholic traditions have emphasized the indissolubility of marriage,
and have ruled out the possibility of divorce. They
have tended to use nullity procedures to deal with
broken marriages. The Reformed traditions have
tended, on the other hand, to see the call to the per-

manence of marriage as a moral ideal, but have recognized that in a fallen world, some marriages sadly are broken, and divorce may be a responsible lesser-evil choice in a flawed situation.

Both of these are examples in which Christian people have learned that there are conscientious differences of view. It has been important for each to give the other freedom of conscience. Some other issues have been the cause of dissension between Christian churches: whether or not oil is used for anointing during baptism; whether infants may properly be baptized or not; whether the Church may or should have bishops as an order of ordained ministry; whether or not women may be ordained priest. These and many other issues have created division and dissension between Christian people. There is an important discussion to be had as to which of these matters are essential to the Church – 'fundamentals' of the faith and of the gospel, and which, though we may believe them to make for the Church's well-being, are matters on which we can give one another freedom of conscience.

Freedom in Truth

For some people, as we remarked briefly earlier, freedom might mean freedom from a painful hurting memory from the past, something which has been a depressing burden for many years, or perhaps something which has come to light later in life, having been buried for a long time. The various ministries which focus on 'healing of memories' seem to be something to do with casting our care on to God, for he cares for us (see 1 Peter 5.7). It is a process of allowing God's liberating Spirit to penetrate deep into our conscious and unconscious minds and bring the freedom of Christ's healing touch to wounded places. There are clearly many cautions to be expressed, false hopes can be raised, unrealizable expectancies can sometimes be offered. But there are many who in their own experience have discovered substantial release in their inner heart through the liberating love of Christ ministered to them through the prayer of others.

St John's Gospel also speaks about 'the truth' which 'sets free' (John 8.32). As we said earlier, some of us carry in our minds patterns of thoughts and responses which actually hold us in the trap of anxiety or depression. To discover a more appropriate way of thinking about ourselves and our world, which is part of what some of the cognitive therapies offer, may enable us to live more fully in the truth which can set free. Particularly for Christian people, this would involve what St Paul calls 'the renewing of our minds' (Romans 12.2) and bringing our thoughts 'captive to the obedience of Christ' (2 Corinthians 10.5) – finding, in other words, that 'captivity' to Christ is a liberation from destructive ways of thinking and behaving.

Personal, social and political freedoms are all part of the passover gospel. From slavery, bondage and from oppressions of many sorts, the God of the Exodus, whose justice and mercy are seen together in the passover lamb, opens the way for liberty. There is not only a freedom from, but equally important is the question: freedom for?

In Bunyan's classic story, *Pilgrim's Progress*, there is scene in which Christian brings the burden of his sins to the cross of Christ, and as he looks at the cross, his burden rolls off his back and he can stand up straight for the rest of his journey to the celestial city. It is a picture Bunyan uses to depict how Christ can bring liberty. The trouble with too many of us is that we then pick up our burdens, put them back on our shoulders and carry them with us as before. Where the Spirit of the Lord is there is liberty!

* * *

For Further Reflection

Jesus went to Nazareth where he had been brought up, and on the Sabbath day he went into the synagogue, as was his custom. And he stood up to read. The scroll of the prophet Isaiah was handed to him. Unrolling it, he found the place where it was written,

'The Spirit of the Lord is on me,
because he has anointed me
to preach good news to the poor.
He has sent me to proclaim freedom for the prisoners
and recovery of sight for the blind,
to release the oppressed,
to proclaim the year of the Lord's favour.'

Then he rolled up the scroll, gave it back to the attendant and sat down. The eyes of everyone in the synagogue were fastened on him, and he said to them, 'Today this scripture is fulfilled in your hearing' (Luke 4.16–21).

* * *

The Lord is the Spirit, and where the Spirit of the Lord is, there is freedom' (2 Corinthians 3.17).

A PRAYER

Eternal God, who art the light of the minds that know thee, the joy of the hearts that love thee, and the strength of the wills that serve thee: grant us so to know thee that we may truly love thee, and so to love thee that we may fully serve thee, whom to serve is perfect freedom, in Jesus Christ our Lord.

after St Augustine

* * *

EASTER WINGS

Lord, who createdst man in wealth and store,
Though foolishly he lost the same,
Decaying more and more,
Till he became
Most poor:
With thee
O let me rise
As larks, harmoniously,
And sing this day thy victories:
Then shall the fall further the flight in me.

My tender age in sorrow did begin:
And still with sicknesses and shame
Thou didst so punish sin,
That I became
Most thin.
With thee
Let me combine
And feel this day thy victory:
For, if I imp[4] my wing on thine,
Affliction shall advance the flight in me.

George Herbert (1593–1633)

SOME QUESTIONS

1. People can be oppressed politically, socially, personally, through poverty, illness, social injustice ... What part do we, or does our church, play in bringing something of God's liberation to people who are oppressed? Prayer? Action? Giving? Political concern? What else might be appropriate?

2. Are there any areas of our life in which we have discovered something of God's freedom and liberation? Can we name them?

3. Are there any areas of our life in which we believe it is still important to be 'set free'? Can we 'cast our anxieties on to God, for he cares for us'? Perhaps we may need to talk these things through with someone?

* * *

And can it be, that I should gain
An interest in the Saviour's blood?
Died he for me, who caused His pain –
For me, who Him to death pursued?
Amazing love! how can it be
That thou, my God, shouldst die for me?

'Tis mercy all! The Immortal dies:
Who can explore His strange design?
In vain the firstborn seraph tries
To sound the depths of love divine.
'Tis mercy all! Let earth adore,
Let angel minds inquire no more.

He left His Father's throne above –
So free, so infinite His grace –
Emptied Himself of all but love,
And bled for Adam's helpless race:
'Tis mercy all, immense and free;
For, O my God, it found out me!

Long my imprisoned spirit lay[5]
Fast bound in sin and nature's night;
Thine eye diffused a quickening ray –
I woke, the dungeon flamed with light;
My chains fell off, my heart was free,
I rose, went forth, and followed Thee.

No condemnation now I dread;
Jesus, and all in Him, is mine!
Alive in Him, my living Head,
And clothed in righteousness divine,
Bold I approach the eternal throne,
And claim the crown, through Christ my own.

Charles Wesley (1707–88)

THREE

The Sacrificial Lamb

We are exploring some of the Old Testament pictures of the lamb which, like lantern-slides together in a projector, can produce a composite image. We have seen how the lamb in the story of Abraham and Isaac indicates something of God's unexpected yet gracious provision. Then we saw how the passover lamb speaks of liberation. In this third chapter, the theme is forgiveness, and the lamb is the one that comes at the centre of Old Testament sacrifices. We will think about guilt and about forgiveness, and explore how the death of Christ brings to us forgiveness from God.

Guilt

I remember being at a large party some years ago and overhearing a conversation in which one middle-aged gentleman was trying to persuade another to enter a deal with him. It would involve buying up some products on the cheap and then reselling them, relabelled, at some considerable profit. He had access to the goods; a friend of a friend would help with the printing. It would simply mean a bending of the law here, an ignoring of a regulation there. It would only be slightly risky, provided they kept their nerve. I have not forgotten the reply: 'No, thank you, Reg. I would rather go to sleep with a clear conscience.'

On another occasion, a television producer recounted to me how he had been speaking at a lunch meeting of business people, executives, politicians, financiers and others – all Christians – and how he took the opportunity to ask them to explain what difference their faith made to their work. His audience were somewhat surprised, some even embarrassed. He pressed the question: 'In the way you do your job, what difference is there between you and your colleagues who are not Christians?' Eventually one of his hearers ventured an answer. It was one word: 'guilt'.

We may reflect on whether other colleagues were themselves as free from the consciousness of guilt as the Christian respondent implied. But the television producer was surely right to wonder what sort of faith it was that left its adherents simply feeling guilty.

Guilt is one of the ever present features of human life in this fallen world. It is something which at times all of us feel. Some of us become so crippled with guilt that we seem not to have the freedom to enjoy life any more. The sense that 'the joy of the Lord is our strength' gets lost in the stresses of coping with guilty feelings.

Guilt and Guilty Feelings

We need to distinguish guilty feelings, however, from moral guilt. The former is the sense of being ill at ease with our conscience; the latter is the fact of being morally in the wrong in relation to some standard of what is right. Now it is possible to feel guilty without being morally guilty. A great deal of pastoral ministry, especially in the area of sexuality, seems to have to do with helping people to see their burden of guilt as unnecessary, and more the product of unhelpful learning experiences of one sort or another than of any true moral guilt. Some people develop an over-scrupulous conscience. I remember a girl at college who used to place a handkerchief on her head when she said grace at meals, because she thought St Paul's teaching that women should cover their heads when praying still applied today, and though she was not sure that grace 'counted' as prayer, she covered her head 'just in case'.

Some people's experiences of life lead them to assume that if something is wrong, the wrong must be in them or be their fault. Often this can come from very critical voices constantly telling them off and putting them down in their early years. Other people are so afraid of overstepping a line that they hardly step anywhere, and are trapped in a cautious, frightened approach to life which is far from joyous or liberating. The sixteenth-century theologian John Calvin has an illustration of this:

When consciences once ensnare themselves, they enter a long and inextricable maze not easy to get out of. If a man begins to doubt whether he may use linen for sheets, shirts, handkerchiefs and napkins, he will afterwards be uncertain also about hemp; finally doubt will arise even over tow. ... If a man should consider daintier food unlawful, in the end he will not be at peace with God when he eats black bread. ... If he boggles at sweet wine, he will not with clear conscience drink even flat wine, and finally he will not dare to touch water,

if sweeter and cleaner than other water. To sum
up, he will come to the point of considering it
wrong to step upon a straw across his path.[1]

It is quite possible, therefore, to feel guilty without
being guilty! On the other hand, it is possible to be
guilty in a moral sense without feeling guilty. We
can blunt our consciences, and persuade ourselves
that what we really know to be wrong is actually in
our special case excusable or even justifiable. Cross-
ing moral boundaries which are given (in our
society, or in our Christian tradition) for our protection and our well-being becomes easier, but with the
loss of those boundaries comes also a diminution of
our moral character. We can deal with our real guilt
by denial. There are, for example, a range of psychological mechanisms which we sometimes use for
refusing to acknowledge unwelcome feelings. We
might suppress them (and then we might find that
they show themselves unexpectedly, when we feel
very strongly about things which we would not
expect in themselves to provoke such strong feelings
– the deep feelings really belong elsewhere). Or we
might project them on to someone else, and treat
the other person as though they were the guilty
ones.

Another way we can deal with guilt is the
common ploy of blame-shifting. We can very
quickly refuse to take responsibility for our choices
or our actions. We see ourselves as victims, like the
cartoon poster which announced 'Humpty Dumpty
was pushed.' Or as the little girl explained to her
mother, on being caught with her hand in the biscuit
tin, 'It is not me, it is my glands.' Or we can put

blame onto others, as Adam did in the Garden of Eden: 'The woman you put here with me – she gave me some fruit from the tree, and I ate it.' So did Eve: 'The serpent deceived me, and I ate.'

But the problem of guilt remains. Guilt in relationship can only be atoned by a process of acknowledging that wrong has occurred, and then by the one who has been wronged refusing to allow the wrong to destroy the relationship. And the Christian word for that process is forgiveness.

Old Testament Sacrifices

This brings us to another of the Old Testament symbols and stories in which a lamb is used to demonstrate something about God, in this case God's forgiveness. In the sacrificial system of the Old Testament, the lamb shows the costliness of being forgiven as well as the freedom of divine grace.

Detailed regulations are provided for a person who wishes to receive the forgiveness of God and have his or her relationship to God restored. In one form they are illustrated in the book of Leviticus. A whole range of offerings are prescribed to deal with a number of eventualities. A cereal offering (Leviticus 2.1) could be made as a response of gratitude to God for his grace. A peace offering (Leviticus 3.1ff.) was an optional sacrifice sometimes linked with making a vow. Purification offerings, or sin offerings, were made (Leviticus 4.1ff.) after a person had committed a deliberate or inadvertent sin. But behind, and over, all these was an offering which made atonement for sin in a general sense, an offering which demonstrated how things are made right again between God and human beings after their relationship has been spoiled through sin. This was the whole burnt offering, offered daily in the court of the tabernacle. It involved a perfect animal, sometimes a bull, sometimes a goat, sometimes birds such as turtle doves or pigeons, But it was often a lamb.

One particular set of instructions for a worshipper is expressed like this:

> If the offering is a burnt offering from the flock, from either the sheep or the goats, he is to offer a male without defect. He is to slaughter it at the north side of the altar before the Lord, and Aaron's sons the priests shall sprinkle its blood against the altar on all sides. He is to cut it into pieces, and the priest shall arrange them, including the head and the fat, on the burning wood that is on the altar. He is to wash the inner parts and the legs with water, and the priest is to bring all of it and burn it on the altar. It is a burnt offering, an offering made by fire, an aroma pleasing to the Lord' (Leviticus 1.10–13).

The worshipper was actively involved in giving, preparing and sacrificing the animal. In many of the other sacrifices, the priest would have taken care of the slaughter, but in the burnt offering, the worshipper kills the animal himself.

To our minds, animal sacrifice often creates a picture both barbaric and primitive. But at the stage in the life of the people of God when they were wanderers in the desert, living in tents, much of their livelihood depending on flocks and herds, the giving of an animal to the Lord represented the giving of the most essential part of the self.

A Total Offering

In his commentary on Leviticus, Gordon Wenham writes:

> Using a little imagination every reader of the OT soon realizes that these ancient sacrifices were very moving occasions. They make modern church services seem tame and dull by comparison. ... The ancient worshipper ... was actively involved in the worship. He had to choose an unblemished animal from his own flock, bring it to the sanctuary, kill it and dismember it with his own hands, then watch it go up in smoke before his very eyes. He was convinced that something very significant was achieved through these acts, and knew that his relationship with God was profoundly affected by this sacrifice.[2]

Wenham goes on to suggest that, because they understood its purpose so well, what we have in Leviticus is mostly just the rubrics for the ritual – the prayers and the meanings are not recorded. However, there are some hints in Leviticus 1 which point to the meaning of the burnt offering. Wenham draws out four. The fact that the animal had to be perfect indicated the offering's importance. The general aim of the sacrifice is 'that he will be acceptable to the Lord' (Leviticus 1.3). In other words, the goal is peace with God. The language of 'an aroma pleasing to the Lord' suggests that the sacrifice soothes the Lord; God's hostility against sin is soothed by the offering of a pleasingly smelling sacrifice. Of crucial importance are the words: the offering 'shall be accepted on his behalf to make atonement for him' (Leviticus 1.4).

As well as the purpose noticed by some other commentators that the burnt offering is an act of consecration, an act of homage, the giving of a gift to God, Wenham and others argue that the burnt offering also, and centrally, makes atonement. When human beings are reminded of their sins, the burnt offering brings sinful people and a holy God into peaceful coexistence again.

So here was an act of the will which could symbolize total consecration. For the worshippers, the flocks were all they had: their companions, their work, their food, their sustenance, their future. It was all this that was offered. The worshipper chose one of the best and offered it to God. And the lamb was not taken along for the ride and then taken home again. It was given totally, wholly, without any reserve, without anything left. No half measures. The sacrificial lamb represented the laying down of life in death. And its purpose was so that life could go on, and be renewed and restored. Death releases the power of life. After the sacrifice of the whole burnt offering, the worshipper could hold his head high again before God at peace. As our Christian hymn puts it: 'ransomed, healed, restored, forgiven'.

In the whole burnt offering, the sacrificial lamb meant: first, a real desire for communion with God; second, a willingness to give the whole of one's self to God; and then third, a willingness to allow God's generous forgiveness to enter one's life.

And this came about, as we saw in the story of Abraham, through a life laid down as the means by which new life could go on. As we said earlier, this is one of the principles of creation itself. When new forms of life emerge in the evolutionary process, they are dependent on other life for their survival. Creation itself involves a cost of life, so that there can be new life.

As we noted before, this is a principle we see in human relationships also. We speak of sacrifice when we give in a way that takes something of our very selves for the enhancement of the lives of others. When a parent gives something of themselves for the sake of their child, that is sacrifice. When nurses keep on going back again and again into the refugee camps which became the war zones in Rwanda for the sake of the survival and health of others, that is a sacrifice. When someone puts his reputation on the line for the sake of others, for the sake of truth, despite hostility and ridicule that can be a sacrifice. When Oates made his decision to walk from Scott's tent that was a supreme self-sacrifice. And according to the fourth Gospel, Jesus gave us these words himself: 'Greater love has no-one than this, that one lay down his life for his friends' (John 15.13).

We have moved from the blood and the smell in the desert to speaking of love. And the reason we can do so without incongruity is that the Exodus event which we explored earlier, God's redeeming event, of which the whole elaborate sacrificial system was a constant reminder, was a supreme demonstration that God was on their side. God had not let them down, God loved Israel as his firstborn son.

And that imagery of sacrifice is powerfully taken up in the New Testament to express the self-offering, self-sacrificing love of God which we see in the death of Jesus, in total consecration, on the cross. Whereas the Old Testament sacrifices could not actually do anything about sin – the worshipper had to come back again and again – the death of Jesus Christ is the reality towards which both the Exodus and the sacrifices of Leviticus point us.

The whole purpose of the letter to the Hebrews is to make this point:

> Day after day every priest stands and performs his religious duties; again and again he offers the same sacrifices, which can never take away sins. But when this priest [Christ] had offered for all time one sacrifice for sins, he sat down at the right hand of God (Hebrews 10.11–12).

Forgiveness

We need now to take stock in more detail of what 'forgiveness' means. Surprisingly, forgiveness is a term which hardly ever features in psychological or psychiatric textbooks. And yet as guilt is a near universal phenomenon, forgiveness is a universal need.

The Christian understanding of human life reminds us that all of us constantly need the forgiveness of God. This is the reason why the daily office in our prayer books begins with the confession of sin. It is not there to make us feel bad as we try to dredge up every little wrong thought we have had during the past day or past week. It is to remind us that we stand before God in worship only on the basis of his forgiveness and merciful grace. It is also there to remind us that, this side of heaven, we will to some extent, always get things wrong.

I once came across a version of the Ten Commandments, which were expressed in reverse – in negative terms – as 'the ten commandments of self-defeat'. They were depicted as the devil's instructions for ensuring fear, worry, anxiety and depression on the earth. One of the devil's commandments of self-defeat reads 'Thou shalt never make mistakes.' Of course we shall make mistakes. I will hurt you, you will hurt me. There will be disappointment and frustration. There will be failure. Faith in God is no protection against failure, suffering and a sense that everything is all wrong.

But forgiveness is a way of saying that life can still go on. Forgiveness does not pretend that things are not wrong. It does not say: 'There, there it does not matter.' Forgiveness does not live the lie of saying everything is fine when in fact a person is hurting because wrong things have been done and said. But forgiveness is a way of rebuilding life and relationships in spite of wrong, and in the light of wrong, in the most creative way possible. Forgiveness is not about brushing things under the carpet. It acknowledges where wrong has occurred and looks it full in the face, but also says that in grace the one who is wronged will not allow the wrong for ever to get in the way of the relationship being restored. Forgiveness is costly, but can be healing.

This is the rich gift which the burnt offerings in Leviticus point towards.

The Law of Retaliation

Much of contemporary society is built upon the law of retaliation: 'You owe, so you must pay.' This quickly becomes the law of bearing grudges, holding resentments, standing on rights, exposing others' failures to ridicule. It is a law from which the Christian family is not immune. Too quickly we react with the authoritarian demand, or by putting one another into categories, or by refusing to let the other person be themselves, because they have offended in some way. Wherever it is found, and even if wrong has truly been done, the law of retaliation can only be destructive. In many human situations, for example for people who may have been sexually abused, the deep feelings of the need for revenge, justice, retribution, are sometimes all too powerfully present – and they can be destructive. This is crippling and stifling to the freedom of love.

By contrast, the gospel tells us of something more positive, more creative, more joyous, though much more costly: the healing power of forgiveness. That is not to say that to deal with painful feelings for someone who has been abused is ever easy or painless. On the contrary, it can be a hard journey of recovery, sometimes later on in life, and usually needing specialist counselling help. But there are many examples of people who have found or are finding help on the way towards moving away from the law of retaliation and retribution.

Forgiveness also breaks down idealizations; it reminds me that both I and you are neither devil nor angel, but sinful and fallible human beings trying to live for Christ, with a lot of the life of Adam still there, but in grace seeking to grow and to change. That is why the writer of the letter to the Ephesians calls on the church to 'put up with one another in love' (Ephesians 4.2: 'bearing with one another').

Forgiveness is constantly creative of new beginnings. How often because someone has fallen into what we think is error, we are ready to write them off. They may have made an error, but God's grace does not write them off.

Forgiveness can be healing, but as we have said, forgiveness is costly. It cost the whole of the precious lamb for the worshipper. It cost Hosea the sacrifice of going out searching for his adulterous wife, finding her up for sale in the market place, and nonetheless bringing her home. It was to cost Jesus Christ no less than the giving of his life.

The Sacrifice of Christ

It is to illustrate the costliness of Christ's self-giving that the New Testament applies to him much of the Old Testament imagery of the sacrificial lamb. This is particularly true of the letter to the Hebrews. There it is made clear that the Old Testament sacrificial system is a shadow. The reality of which this is a shadow is seen in the life and death of Jesus. The Old Testament sacrifices foreshadow the one sacrifice for sins for ever, which is how the writer to the Hebrews understands the death of Christ. By his own will he laid down his life: 'By that will, we have been made holy through the sacrifice of the body of Jesus Christ once for all' (Hebrews 10.10).

The letter goes on immediately to indicate how the sacrificial death of Jesus opens up a new way of

life for Christian believers. Guilt is removed and
consciences can be cleaned. And it is a way of life
which is meant to be shared. In one paragraph, filled
with Old Testament imagery, we read:

> Therefore, since we have confidence to enter the
> Most Holy Place by the blood of Jesus, by a new
> and living way opened for us through the curtain,
> that is, his body, and since we have a great priest
> over the house of God, let us draw near to God
> with a sincere heart in full assurance of faith,
> having our hearts sprinkled to cleanse us from a
> guilty conscience and having our bodies washed
> with pure water. Let us hold unswervingly to the
> hope we profess, for he who promised is faithful.
> And let us consider how we may spur one another
> on towards love and good deeds. Let us not give
> up meeting together, as some are in the habit of
> doing, but let us encourage one another – and all
> the more as you see the Day approaching
> (Hebrews 10.19–25).

So the thinking is clear: God's forgiveness of us,
through the costly self-giving of his sacrificial lamb,
is meant to lead to mutual fellowship and acceptance
within the community.

Forgiveness in Practice

How can forgiveness be applied in modern life?

FORGIVENESS IN PERSONAL RELATIONSHIPS
Let us focus first of all on the *interpersonal dimensions*
to forgiveness; that is forgiving other people, and

forgiving myself. One of the New Testament parables is told by Jesus in response to Peter's question 'Lord, how many times shall I forgive my brother when he sins against me?' (Matthew 18.21).

Jesus compares the kingdom of heaven to a king who wished to settle accounts with his officials, one of whom owed him a massive debt and could not pay. The official implored the king for patience, and the king out of compassion released him and forgave him the debt. That same official, however, refused similar compassion to a fellow worker who in his turn owned him a trifling few pence. The official returned to the law of retaliation: you owe, so you must pay! The king was understandably enraged at this, and delivered the official to the jailers. Clearly the refusal to display forgiveness to one of his fellows demonstrated that this official had not properly understood and received the forgiveness offered by his lord. Jesus' comment is hard: 'This is how my heavenly Father will treat each of you unless you forgive your brother from your heart' (Matthew 18.35).

Forgiveness is thus an act of will to refuse to stand by the law of retaliation, and a determination to reshape the future of the relationship as creatively as possible despite the wrong and the hurt.

There is an instructive example of forgiveness in one of the therapeutic journals.[3] It tells the story of a bright, intelligent, hysterical girl aged twenty-five with a great deal of anger about her upbringing. There had been much trauma in her early life, but also her own learned responses had become increasingly aggressive, causing people to turn away from her. Through sustained therapy, she came to the point of understanding something of the kind of upbringing her own parents had received. 'With this she was able to see that no less than herself, no less than everyone else in the world, her parents were inevitably caught in the effects of their life experiences and possessed both good and bad qualities.' This realization led to a change in attitude in the girl. She abandoned blaming, accepted responsibility for her own behaviour, recognized the real, impartial, impersonality of much human suffering and, with tenderness and some ruefulness, forgave her parents. She then fell in love, and shortly afterwards, married.

Some people also use the term 'forgiveness' of themselves. To come to an appropriate realization of one's own ambiguous state – partly good and partly bad; to refuse to accept an inappropriate burden of guilt; to cease to blame oneself for things for which one is not responsible; to recover a proper sense of self-esteem and self-acceptance: all this is part of the meaning of forgiveness. Many of us need more help in this area of life than we sometimes like to admit.

FORGIVENESS IN SOCIETY

Second, at the *community* level, what would forgiveness imply? My television producer friend wondered how forgiveness could find its way into the thinking and working practices of the Christian business people to whom he was speaking, to move them from stopping simply at 'guilt'. The law of retaliation and resentment can too easily colour community life. Many of the tabloid newspapers feed the pressure in society for exposing as many faults in public figures as we can. The misdemeanours of a person in public life – often many years ago – are made into headlines, sometimes into films. A person who went wrong many years ago, but who repented of it, tried to put right the wrong, sought to forget it, and has for many years lived a useful and good life of social service can suddenly find his past paraded before him and before the world in the sensationalist media. 'You did wrong', they cry, 'and you must always pay for it; always be reminded of it.' How much more generous, more creative, if public opinion could instead be helped to make the response of forgiveness.

A POLITICS OF FORGIVENESS?

At the harder *international* level, could there be such a thing as a *politics of forgiveness*? For example do British international policies tell the world that above all things Britain seeks justice in international affairs? Or do they foster the notion of bare power and the law of retaliation? At the height of the cold war, Britain's posture seemed to be: 'We threaten to be devastatingly cruel to you if you provoke us far enough.'

What would a politics of forgiveness look like? It would certainly acknowledge the reality of evil in the world, but it would seek for ways of responding to wrong in a way that is creative of new possibilities. A politics of forgiveness is not concerned with peace at any price, nor with a destructive intention to destroy those we think of as our enemies. It is concerned, rather, with a willingness to take the costly path of trying to reshape the future in the light of wrong in the most creative way possible. President Mandela and Archbishop Tutu in the new South Africa seem to provide shining examples of this creative possibility. But it is not without cost.

The Cost

The costliness of atonement is stressed in some of the
'theories' of atonement which have reached prominence in the Christian church at different times. In
Anselm's day – the eleventh century – he thought in
the categories of feudal lords, the homage that was
due to them by private citizens, and the need for
satisfaction to be made in response to anything that
harmed the kingdom, Anselm expressed the meaning
of the death of Christ in terms of the restoration of
God's honour. Sin against God is very serious.
Human beings should provide the appropriate satisfaction, but they are unable to. Only God can do
that. That is why God has to become man in order,
as man, to satisfy the honour of God. These are not
categories of thought we use these days, but one
feature of Anselm's exposition which is missing from
some other accounts is the seriousness of sin and the
need for costly sacrifice to deal with it.

Another theory, which came to prominence in the
writing of some of the Reformers, notably John
Calvin, used the legal categories with which Calvin
was professionally familiar, and understood sin not so
much in damaging God's honour as in breaking
God's law. The penalty for lawbreaking has to be
paid. Calvin understood Jesus Christ as bearing the
penalty on behalf of sinful human beings, standing in
their place as their substitute. This view has been cri-
ticized as offering a sort of legal fiction which
appears less than just: Jesus, the sinless bears the
penalty for sin; we, the guilty, go free.

If we can move beyond the legal categories of lawbreaking and law courts, however, it cannot be

denied that in some of the Old Testament imagery of the lamb there is some understanding of substitution. The lamb dies in place of Isaac. The lamb dies in place of the Israelites in Egypt. The lamb dies in the burnt offering, so that the worshipper can find peace again with God. That exchange is also picked up in the New Testament, not using Calvin's legal language so much as the interpersonal language of 'reconciliation'. 'God made him [Christ] who had no sin to be sin for us, so that in him we might become the righteousness of God' (2 Corinthians 5.21). Whatever that mysterious text points to in the nature of God, it has resonances with the lambs of sacrifice in the Old Testament. From the sacrificial lamb we are given a picture of the possibilities of restored relationships.

The New Testament builds on this picture. We realize that forgiveness and living in grace is meant to be shared. It involves self-giving, consecration, a willingness to lay down things as precious as life itself for the sake of new life. The message of the gospel is that it is through costly vulnerability and self-giving love that life can go on, and be made new. That is part of the reason the New Testament calls Jesus 'the Lamb of God'.

* * *

For Further Reflection

Out of the depths I cry to you, O Lord;
O Lord, hear my voice.
Let your ears be attentive to my cry for mercy.
If you, O Lord, kept a record of sins,
O Lord, who could stand?
But with you there is forgiveness; therefore you are
    feared.

I wait for the Lord, my soul waits,
and in his word I put my hope.
My soul waits for the Lord more than watchmen
  wait for the morning,
more than watchmen wait for the morning.

O Israel, put your hope in the Lord!
for with the Lord is unfailing love
and with him is full redemption.
He himself will redeem Israel from all their sins.
  (Psalm 130).

*   *   *

When they came to the place which is called The
Skull, there they crucified him, along with the
criminals – one on his right, the other on his left.
Jesus said, 'Father, forgive them, for they do not
know what they are doing.' And they divided up
his clothes by casting lots. The people stood
watching, and the rulers even sneered at him.
They said, 'He saved others; let him save himself if
he is the Christ of God, the Chosen One.' The
soldiers also came up and mocked him. They
offered him wine vinegar and said, 'If you are the
King of the Jews, save yourself.' There was a
written notice above him, which read: THIS IS THE
KING OF THE JEWS.

One of the criminals who hung there hurled
insults at him: 'Aren't you the Christ? Save yourself and us!' But the other criminal rebuked him.
'Don't you fear God,' he said, 'since you are under
the same sentence? We are punished justly, for we
are getting what our deeds deserve. But this man
has done nothing wrong.' Then he said, 'Jesus,

remember me when you come into your
kingdom.' Jesus answered him, 'I tell you the
truth, today you will be with me in paradise.'

(Luke 23.33–43)

PRAYERS

> Cleanse me from my sin, Lord,
> Put thy power within, Lord,
> Take me as I am, Lord,
> And make me all thine own.
> Keep me day by day, Lord,
> Underneath thy sway, Lord,
> Make my heart thy palace,
> And thy royal throne.

Almighty and everlasting God,
you are always more ready to hear than we to pray
and give more than we either desire or deserve.
Pour down upon us the abundance of your mercy,
forgiving us those things of which our conscience is
    afraid,
and giving us those good things which we are not
    worthy to ask
save through the merits and mediation of Jesus
    Christ, your Son our Lord.

from the Gelasian Sacramentary

SOME QUESTIONS

1. Are there any examples in our local community where 'the law of retaliation and retribution' seems to rule? Are there ways in which the power of forgiveness could be brought into that situation?

2. Are there ways in which we can help our families, places of work, church ... towards living out the gospel of forgiveness?

3. In our own lives there are often things which we could 'let go' by forgiving someone, by apologizing, by putting something right, by finding a more creative response, by opening the situation up to God's grace. Sometimes the forgiving process can take a long time. Can we think of some steps which we should be taking in that process now?

> In evil long I took delight,
> Unawed by shame or fear,
> Till a new object struck my sight,
> And stopped my wild career:
>
> I saw One hanging on a Tree
> In agonies and blood,
> Who fix'd his languid eyes on me,
> As near his Cross I stood.
>
> Sure never till my latest breath
> Can I forget that look:
> It seem'd to charge me with his death,
> Though not a word he spoke:

My conscience felt and owned the guilt,
And plunged me in despair;
I saw my sins his blood had spilt,
And helped to nail him there.

Alas! I knew not what I did!
But now my tears are vain:
Where shall my trembling soul be hid?
For I the Lord have slain!

– A second look he gave, which said,
'I freely all forgive;
This blood is for thy ransom paid;
I die, that thou may'st live.'

Thus, while his death my sin displays
In all its blackest hue,
Such is the mystery of grace,
It seals my pardon too.

With pleasing grief, and mournful joy,
My spirit now is fill'd,
That I should such a life destroy, –
Yet live by him I kill'd.

John Newton (1725–1807);
a former slave trader.

FOUR ✥

The Suffering Lamb

Our fourth lantern-slide picture is taken from much later in the Old Testament history. We move now across several centuries to the time of the prophecies recorded in the second half of the book of Isaiah. In chapters 40 to 55 there are a series of poems, written to encourage the people of God during the time of exile away from their own land. Some of these are called the 'Servant Songs' because their central figure is called God's servant. They contain, as we shall see, a strange interweaving of royal power and innocent suffering, of service and authority.

Authority or Power?

The word 'authority' is often confused with the word 'power'. Sometimes they belong together, but sometimes those in 'authority' find that 'power' belongs somewhere else. We sometimes speak of the 'authorities' as the 'powers that be'. Those 'in authority' sometimes are and sometimes are not those who have power to make decisions which affect the lives of others. The word 'power' itself more often than not, suggests 'coercive power'. Sometimes we speak about 'the abuse of power', or say of someone that power 'has gone to his head'. For some people 'power' indicates large impersonal institutions against which we have to fight, and before which we feel helpless. For others, authority is linked with the sort of political power which rules, which leads, which dominates, which is in control. This was the understanding of Jesus' disciples on the day when James and John asked Jesus to grant them positions of authority in his coming kingdom. They were assuming that the authority of Jesus Christ would be demonstrated by the coercive exercise of political power. Yet Jesus' reply reveals how out of touch with the pattern of his kingdom those disciples' questions were:

> You know that those who are regarded as rulers of the Gentiles lord it over them, and their high officials exercise authority over them. Not so with you. Instead, whoever wants to become great among you must be your servant, and whoever wants to be first must be slave of all. For even the Son of Man did not come to be served, but to serve, and to give his life as a ransom for many (Mark 10.43–5ff.).

The authority which Jesus displays is not that of coercive power, but that of service. Service is people-centred, concerned with enhancing human values, opening the way for others to find more liberty, more health, more well-being. In our post-Enlightenment world, one of our inheritances in the area of political and social life is an increasing network of bureaucracy. Some decades ago, the sociologist Max Weber predicted that growing bureaucracy would function in society like 'an iron cage'. The dictatorship of the bureaucrats is increasingly a reality in Western democracies. We hear a great deal about efficiency, about cost-benefit, about profit margins, about management. We find that decisions in what used to be called 'service industries' and 'caring professions' are increasingly dominated by 'management'. We hear much more about management than about service. Ministry becomes administration. The human values and person-centred concerns of the service of our neighbours can very easily get lost in the noise of faxes, computer keyboards and photocopying machines. This is not, of course, to say that management, efficiency and computers cannot aid us in the service of our neighbours – of course they can, and should. It is, however, to say that the authority of economics and and the power of technology, though good servants, can be very oppressive masters.

One example of oppressive technology was described years ago by then American President Eisenhower. He warned against the development of what he called a 'military-industrial complex' – a combination of military technologists and leaders in the defence industries, who together could, if not checked, take over the role of politicians in dictating priorities for action in international conflict and preparation for defence. The power of new military technology might become the driving force for political decision.

We can find another example of oppressive technology in the medical world. It is well known that modern medicine is able to sustain life much longer in many cases than our grandparents could ever have imagined. This has given rise to the possibility of sustaining the functioning of the body by ventilator or other life-support machine, in a way which effectively prolongs the processes of dying. It poses in urgent ways the question of when and where lines are to be drawn between the medical treatment which is appropriate for the living and the medical care which is appropriate for the dying. Some interventions of powerful medical technology may be dehumanizing, prolonging life's length at the expense of the quality of life itself.

The Authority of Service

There is a very different form of authority graphically illustrated in the Fourth Gospel when, on the night on which he was betrayed, Jesus rose from supper and took a towel, poured water into a basin and proceeded to wash his disciples' feet.

> 'Do you understand what I have done for you?' he asked. 'You call me "Teacher" and "Lord"; and rightly so, for that is what I am. Now that I, your Lord and Teacher, have washed your feet, you also should wash one another's feet. I have set you an example that you should do as I have done for you' (John 13.12–14).

St Paul also gives classic expression to this linking of authority with the humility of the servant, in the beautiful hymn he includes in Philippians 2:

> Your attitude should be the same as that of Christ Jesus: Who, being in very nature God, did not consider equality with God something to be grasped, but made himself nothing, taking the very nature of a servant, being made in human likeness. And being found in appearance as a man, he humbled himself and became obedient to death

– even death on a cross! Therefore God exalted
him to the highest place and gave him the name
that is above every name, that at the name of Jesus
every knee should bow, in heaven and on earth
and under the earth, and every tongue confess that
Jesus Christ is Lord, to the glory of God the
Father (Philippians 2.5–11).

This was the pattern of authority through service
which the apostles taught in the churches of the first
century. 'Christ suffered for you, leaving you an
example, that you should follow his steps,' writes
Peter. 'Be shepherds of God's flock that is under
your care, serving as overseers – not because you
must, but because you are willing, as God wants you
to be; not greedy for money, but eager to serve; not
lording it over those entrusted to you, but being
examples to the flock' (1 Peter 2.21; 5.2–3).

The sort of authority prescribed for the Church –
which is characteristic of God's kingdom – is an
authority not of status nor of power, but of service.
The servant is one who is prepared to suffer for the
sake of those he serves.

The Suffering Servant

The classic passage in the Old Testament which illustrates the theme of suffering service is one in which,
once again, we find the imagery of the lamb. It is
found in one of the Servant Songs of the second part
of Isaiah.

The figure of God's Messiah is described as a
servant. His death is spoken of in these terms: 'He

was pierced for our transgressions, he was crushed
for our iniquities ... the Lord has laid on him the
iniquity of us all' (Isaiah 53.5–6).

The servant suffers in the place of the people: 'He
was oppressed and afflicted, yet he did not open his
mouth; he was led like a lamb to the slaughter, and
as a sheep before her shearers is silent, so he did not
open his mouth.'

We have earlier seen how the Old Testament uses
the imagery of the lamb to speak of God's gracious
and surprising provision. We have seen how the lamb
is central to the passover gospel of liberation. We
traced through the sacrificial system to see the function of the death of the lamb in providing a means
for forgiveness and renewed life. And now all these
images come together, and they come together in a
person. Here for the first time in the Old Testament,
the lamb is associated with an individual person.

We need to take some time to explore what Isaiah
says about this most significant person.

The servant, we learn from previous chapters is
God's chosen one in whom God's soul delights. God
has put his Spirit upon him, and he will bring justice
to the nations and establish justice in the earth (Isaiah
42.1ff.).

The servant is then described in national terms:
'Jacob my servant, Israel whom I have chosen' (Isaiah
44.1). The servant is his whole people Israel, those
whom God has redeemed (Isaiah 44.21-2).

The Servant King

In Isaiah 52, the servant is depicted as a single individual in whom all the fortunes of God's people are

embodied. The servant is one in whom the true nature of the people of Israel is summed up and personified. The servant is Israel as she was meant to be. He is the true Israel of God. Isaiah 52.13 describes him in royal terms. 'He will be raised and lifted up and highly exalted.' This is a picture of a royal person in triumphal procession. He will come to Israel as a ruler.

And yet what a king! Many were astonished at his appearance. He is a king in humiliation. Those who see him are startled. Messiah's victory is not an exercise of coercive power. His victory is not military and political; it is a victory in the hearts and minds of people (Isaiah 52.15). The king is a suffering servant.

And so to Isaiah 53:

Who has believed our message and to whom has the arm of the Lord been revealed? He grew up before him like a tender shoot, and like a root out of dry ground. He had no beauty or majesty to attract us to him, nothing in his appearance that we should desire him. He was despised and rejected by men, a man of sorrows, and familiar with suffering. Like one from whom men hide their faces he was despised, and we esteemed him not.

Surely he took up our infirmities and carried our sorrows, yet we considered him stricken by God, smitten by him, and afflicted. But he was pierced for our transgressions, he was crushed for our iniquities; the punishment that brought us peace was upon him, and by his wounds we are healed. We all, like sheep, have gone astray, each of us has turned to his own way; and the Lord has laid on him the iniquity of us all.

He was oppressed and afflicted, yet he did not open his mouth; he was led like a lamb to the slaughter, and as a sheep before her shearers is silent, so he did not open his mouth. By oppression and judgment he was taken away. And who can speak of his descendants? For he was cut off from the land of the living; for the transgression of my people he was stricken. He was assigned a grave with the wicked, and with the rich in his death, though he had done no violence, nor was any deceit in his mouth.

Yet it was the Lord's will to crush him and cause him to suffer, and though the Lord makes his life a guilt offering, he will see his offspring and prolong his days, and the will of the Lord will prosper in his hand. After the suffering of his soul, he will see the light of life and be satisfied; by his knowledge my righteous servant will justify many, and he will bear their iniquities. Therefore I will give him a portion among the great, and he will divide the spoils with the strong, because he poured out his life unto death, and was numbered with the transgressors. For he bore the sins of many, and made intercession for the transgressors.

In this chapter, the watchmen of Jerusalem feel justified in trying to explain how the community have failed to recognize their king. Who has believed their message? (verse 1) The messianic king was not recognized because there was no outward show of royal power (verse 2). He was not like King David, who was described as being of beautiful countenance. This king had 'no beauty or majesty to attract us to him'. He was despised and rejected by men, a man of sorrows and acquainted with grief.

> Surely he took up our infirmities and carried our sorrows, yet we considered him stricken by God, smitten by him, and afflicted. But he was pierced for our transgressions, he was crushed for our iniquities; the punishment that brought us peace was upon him, and by his wounds we are healed.

Then comes the reference to lambs and sheep: we are like sheep, he is like an innocent lamb.

> We all, like sheep, have gone astray, each of us has turned to his own way; and the Lord has laid on him the iniquity of us all. He was oppressed and afflicted, yet he did not open his mouth; he was led like a lamb to the slaughter, and as a sheep before her shearers is silent, so he did not open his mouth.

Not Like a King!

God has taken away from the kingly Messiah any possible semblance of earthly political power. In no way did he look like a king. And this was precisely to show that his kingdom was the rule of God first and foremost in the hearts and minds of people. There are, of course, social and political implications of the kingly rule of God in people's hearts and minds. But the point of this paragraph is to emphasize that the servant's work is not the wielding of power, but the bearing of griefs and carrying of sorrows. He serves his people as king, not by lording it over them, but by his identification in their needs and their pains. The servant of the Lord was smitten by God and afflicted. But his suffering is his service. He was wounded for our transgressions and bruised for our iniquities; upon him was the chastisement which made us whole; and with his stripes we are healed.

The grief and the pain are then extraordinarily explained not as a tragic failure of the servant who somehow slipped outside the control of God. 'It was the Lord's will to crush him, and cause him to suffer' (Isaiah 53.10). In other words, God himself is intimately involved in the suffering of his servant, whose death is ordained as the means by which the people may know his kingly rule in their lives and so be made whole.

What strange power is this! – the power of suffering service. Through the self-giving love of one who is unjustly bruised and chastised, many are accounted righteous (Isaiah 53.11). This new David – the prototype shepherd king – now gives his life for the sheep. And in the prophet Isaiah's mind, the imagery of the lamb is most appropriate. 'He was oppressed and afflicted, yet he did not open his mouth; he was led like a lamb to the slaughter, and as a sheep before her shearers is silent, so he did not open his mouth' (Isaiah 53.7).

There are resonances here with the sacrificial lamb of the day of atonement; there are overtones of the passover lamb through whose death the people are liberated. These earlier images come together, and do so in a person. Here, we may well believe, is part of the reason for John the Baptist's choice of words to point to Jesus: 'Behold! the Lamb of God who takes away the sin of the world.'

Ken and Andrew

One contemporary example illustrates the cost and power of suffering service. Ken and Andrew were friends. When a vacancy occurred in the business of which Andrew was managing director, he invited Ken to join the staff. What was not clear then was that what Andrew really wanted was a 'yes-man', and he wrongly thought that he could trade on Ken's friendship to guarantee his unqualified support. Soon after Ken arrived it became clear that Andrew's style of leadership was domineering; he gave all his attention to the business, and expected one hundred and fifty per cent from all the staff. Ken was much more people-centred, and found that he became the one that other staff complained to about the pressures Andrew was putting them all under.

Eventually Ken felt that it was his responsibility to confront Andrew, and let him know about the feelings of the other staff, and to ask him to be a little less demanding. When he did, all hell broke loose. Andrew, who was in fact becoming increasingly jealous of Ken's good relationships with the rest of the staff, turned from being a supportive friend to being an undermining enemy. He refused to accept the criticisms, and instead suggested that Ken was inciting the rest of the staff against him. Ken made several attempts to defuse the situation, but to no avail. Andrew used his power to make Ken's life very difficult. In fact he drew some of Andrew's pressure on the others to himself, and their working conditions did improve somewhat. The other staff were caught in their respect for Ken, on the one hand, and yet the need to protect their own skins, on the other. If Andrew was like this to a friend, what would he do to them?

Ken reluctantly came to the conclusion that he had no option but to resign. Others said he should have taken another course. He should have shouted back and stood up for himself. He should have taken the matter to court. He should have asked the other staff to side with him and make Andrew's increasingly unprofessional behaviour public. In fact he quietly resigned.

There were many times when he had been tempted to fight back and justify himself, or simply fight for justice. But that, he felt, would have been to play by Andrew's rules. What sustained him was the phrase from 1 Peter 2 describing the example of Christ: 'When they hurled their insults at him, he did not retaliate.' It hurt not to fight back. It hurt simply to accept injustice. It hurt to bear unfair criticism. He realized that this would not be right for everyone: each situation is different. But for him, he believed that entrusting himself 'to him who judges justly' meant that this was the right course for him to take, in the faith that eventually the truth would emerge, and would set free. When the truth did come out, Andrew realized that his attitude could not be repeated. Ken prays that one day Andrew will be healed. Was he right? His was a costly action of self-sacrificing service, a deliberate decision not to play by the rules of coercive power. It was costly; but it may yet prove to be health-giving.

Power and Service within the Church

Christian ministry within the Church is not immune

from struggles for power. Various factions within the
Church can be tempted, out of a belief that they are
standing for truth, to make bids for power which in
reality derive from fear and insecurity. A willingness
to be vulnerable for the sake of Christ can be mis-
construed as weakness. Power struggles for leadership
within church congregations can be translated into
terms of 'respect for authority' or the 'wisdom of
experience'.

Some churches have sought to move from 'One-
Man-Band' patterns of leadership into shared elder-
ships, and sometimes this has led to struggles with
the question of where power and authority actually
lie. Sometimes a charismatic leader will enthuse the
congregation with his or her own fire and vision,
taking on single-handed the responsibility for the
spiritual health of everyone else. Too frequently such
a person burns out into illness, paranoia or despair.
By contrast, a style of leadership which recognizes
the interconnectedness of relationships within the
'family system' which is the church congregation –
in which ministry is seen not as coercing others but
as serving them, facilitating others' gifts, being one
among many within the Body of Christ – such a
style will not catch the headlines, will not become
known as a 'key' church; but may be nearer to the
heart of the servant Lamb.

Part of the Christian gospel is to display in action,
in lifestyle and in patterns of church life that there is
an alternative to the authority of coercion and domination. The alternative is the authority of love, of
vulnerability, of self-giving, of service. One of the
medieval theories of atonement, from the pen of
Abelard, concentrates on how the cross shows us the

love of God, and inspires in us love in return. It concentrates more subjectively than some of the other 'theories' on the effect of Christ's death upon sinful people, giving them an example of self-giving love. The writer seems to take a similar tack in Hebrews 12:

> Let us throw off everything that hinders and the sin that so easily entangles, and let us run with perseverance the race marked out for us. Let us fix our eyes on Jesus, the author and perfector of our faith, who for the joy set before him endured the cross, scorning its shame, and sat down at the right hand of the throne of God' (Hebrews 12.1–2).

We may wish to say more about the meaning of Christ's death than that it was an example of self-giving, shame-enduring love. There are many other metaphors to use, images to draw on, stories to tell. But the image of the suffering servant is, in its unexpected way, one of the most powerful.

* * *

For Further Reflection

> To this you were called, because Christ suffered for you, leaving you an example, that you should follow in his steps. 'He committed no sin, no deceit was found in his mouth.' When they hurled their insults at him, he did not retaliate; when he suffered, he made no threats. Instead, he entrusted himself to him who judges justly. He himself bore our sins in his body on the tree, so that we might

die to sins and live for righteousness; by his wounds you have been healed. For you were like sheep going astray, but now you have returned to the Shepherd and Overseer of your souls' (1 Peter 2.21–5).

* * *

Then Jesus went with his disciples to a place called Gethsemane, and he said to them, 'Sit here while I go over there and pray.' He took Peter and the two sons of Zebedee along with him and he began to be sorrowful and troubled. Then he said to them, 'My soul is overwhelmed with sorrow to the point of death. Stay here and keep watch with me.' Going a little farther, he fell with his face to the ground and prayed, 'My Father, if it is possible, may this cup be taken from me. Yet not as I will, but as you will.' (Matthew 26. 36–9).

* * *

When Jesus came out wearing the crown of thorns and the purple robe, Pilate said to them, 'Here is the man!' As soon as the chief priests and the officials saw him, they shouted, 'Crucify! Crucify!' But Pilate answered, 'You take him and crucify him. As for me, I find no basis for a charge against him.' The Jews insisted, 'We have a law, and according to that law he must die, because he claimed to be the the Son of God.' When Pilate heard this, he was even more afraid, and he went back inside the palace. 'Where do you come from?' he asked Jesus, but Jesus gave him no answer. 'Do you refuse to speak to me?' Pilate said. 'Don't you realise that I have power either to free you or to crucify you?' Jesus answered, 'You would have no power over me if it were not given to you from above.' ...

So the soldiers took charge of Jesus. Carrying his own cross, he went out to The Place of the Skull (which in Aramaic is called Golgotha). Here they crucified him, and with him two others – one on each side and Jesus in the middle. Pilate had a notice prepared and fastened to the cross. It read JESUS OF NAZARETH, THE KING OF THE JEWS (John 19.5–11; 17–19).

* * *

A PRAYER

We beseech thee, O Lord, remember all for good; have mercy upon all, O God. Remember every soul who, being in any affliction, trouble or agony, stands in need of thy mercy and help, all who are in necessity or distress, all who love or hate us.

Thou, O Lord, art the Helper of the helpless, the Hope of the hopeless, the Saviour of them who are tossed with tempests, the Haven of them who sail; be thou all to all. The glorious majesty of the Lord our God be upon us; prosper thou the work of our hands. Lord, be thou within us to strengthen us, without us to keep us, above us to protect us, beneath us to uphold us, before us to direct us, behind us to keep us from straying, round about us to defend us. Blessed be Thou, O Lord our Father, for ever and ever.

Lancelot Andrewes (1555–1626)

When I consider how my light is spent,
Ere half my days, in this dark world and wide,
And that one talent which is death to hide
Lodged with me useless, though my soul more bent
To serve therewith my Maker, and present
My true account, lest he returning chide,
'Doth God exact day-labour, light denied?'
I fondly ask. But Patience, to prevent
That murmur, soon replies: 'God doth not need
Either man's work or his own gifts; who best
Bear his mild yoke, they serve him best. His state
Is kingly; thousands at his bidding speed,
And post o'er land and ocean without rest;
They also serve who only stand and wait.'

John Milton (1608–74)
Sonnet on His Blindness

SOME QUESTIONS:

1. Many of us find ourselves in roles (in work, family, church, communities) which include some power over the lives of others. How much do we use that power for coercion, how much for service?

2. It is sometimes said 'power has gone to his head' or she 'needs to be taken down a peg or two'. Does their leadership style provoke such reactions? How much is the leader, and how much is resentment and jealousy in others?

3. How far do the patterns of leadership in our church, at all levels, reflect the ministry of the servant king? Do these patterns empower others to fulfil their ministries of service?

4. Look at the story of Ken and Andrew. Would you have done the same as Ken? Was he acting justly? Was he strong or weak? Was he being a doormat, or standing for the truth? What would you have done if you had been Andrew?

* * *

O sacred head, sore wounded,
With grief and shame weighed down!
O kingly head, surrounded
With thorns, thine only crown!
How pale art thou with anguish,
With sore abuse and scorn!
How does that visage languish,
Which once was bright as morn!

O Lord of life and glory,
What bliss till now was thine!
I read the wondrous story;
I joy to call thee mine.
Thy grief and bitter passion
Were all for sinner's gain;
Mine, mine was the transgression,
But thine the deadly pain.

What language shall I borrow
To praise thee, heavenly friend,
For this thy dying sorrow,
Thy pity without end?
Lord, make me thine for ever,
Not let me faithless prove;
O let me never, never
abuse such dying love.

Paul Gerhardt (1607–76),
tr. J. W. Alexander

FIVE

The Victorious Lamb

We have been exploring the sorts of pictures John the Baptist may have had in his mind when he pointed to Jesus and said 'Behold! the Lamb of God who takes away the sins of the world.' In our exploration we have briefly noted various ways in which 'the Lamb of God' points us to ways of understanding the meaning of the death of Christ – theories of the atonement. We have heard echoes of some of the concerns of Anselm for God's honour, of Calvin for God's justice and God's law, of Abelard for God's love. But much more to the fore have been other themes.

Perhaps one of the pictures John the Baptist had in mind – one of the glass lantern-slides in our projector – was the story of Abraham and Isaac. The lamb functioned there as a picture of God's surprising provision, a picture of grace and providence. The paschal lamb of passover night was a powerful symbol in the memory of the people of God's judgement against the false gods of Egypt and God's liberation of Israel from slavery. It spoke of liberty and of obedience. The lambs of sacrifice in the book of Leviticus point us to God's way of dealing with sin and guilt through the gift of forgiveness, and the importance of repentance and consecration. Isaiah's prophecy of the suffering servant who was led like a lamb to the slaughter is a poignant picture of the power of leadership through vulnerability and self-giving. It helped us link together suffering and health. All of these pictures, we have seen, point to aspects of the New Testament understanding of who Jesus is, and what his death means.

Our final chapter picks up a different symbol. We turn now to another ancient Jewish text, the book of Enoch, which doubtless John the Baptist also knew, where the 'lamb' takes on a different role. The lamb here becomes the great horned ram who leads the flock to victory. Was this picture also part of John the Baptist's slide collection? Whether it was or not, it seems very likely that this picture certainly influenced the writer of the New Testament book of Revelation, in which 'the Lamb' becomes 'the Lion', no longer bruised and broken, but glorious in the victory of suffering love. Many of the other themes we have already explored will surface again when we look at the book of Revelation. There grace and liberation, forgiveness and healing are all bound up in the minds of the worshippers with the Lamb on the throne of heaven. For the Christ in glory at the centre of this world's worship is the one who walked this earth in the Judaean desert when John was baptizing, the one to whom John pointed with the words 'Behold! the Lamb of God.'

Victory is also one of the central themes of an extremely influential way of stating the doctrine of the atonement. We find it in some of the earliest theologians in the Christian Church. We find it in the writings of Martin Luther. In the 1930s, a time of much disturbance in Europe, it was revived by the Swedish theologian, Gustav Aulén. His book is called *Christus Victor*.[1] In his death, Christ has won a great victory over all the powers of evil. We find the theme in St Paul's writing, alongside some of the other passages we have already looked at, in this brief paragraph:

> When you were dead in your sins ... God made you alive with Christ. He forgave us all our sins having cancelled the written code, with its regulations, that was against us and that stood opposed to us; he took it away, nailing it to the cross. And having disarmed the powers and authorities, he made a public spectacle of them, triumphing over them by the cross' (Colossians 2.13–15).

Aulén's vision is of a cosmic Christ engaged in cosmic warfare against evil. This is imagery of which the book of Revelation is full, and in a short while we will turn to the last book of the Bible for our final lantern-slide picture of 'the Lamb', to whose glorious throne, we discover, all things are coming.

What Is the World Coming To?

'What is the world coming to?' is a phrase one sometimes hears on the lips of older people, scandalized by the behaviour of the young. Sometimes it is a question asked in puzzlement at our apparent impotence in the face of the constantly changing world scene. It is a question many are asking in the light of the widespread problems of ecological imbalance, of pollution on a global scale. 'What is the world coming to?' is a question asked by thinking people as the older consensus about morality, order and justice gives way to politics by terrorism, government by secrecy, the collapse of any shared agreement about meaning or truth in the cultures of post-modernity.

But it is not a Christian question. A more biblical way of putting the question would be 'To whom is the world coming?' or even 'Who is coming to his world?'

For the question of world history and world destiny in the minds of the writers of the New Testament is not concerned with the operation of market forces, nor simply with the outworking of human selfishness on a global scale. Nor is it abandonment to a blind and perhaps cruel fate. The question of world history and world destiny belong within a faith in God the creator and redeemer of his world. As the old song put it: 'He's got the whole wide world in his hands.'

To be sure, it does not always look like this. As we saw in our discussion of Abraham and Isaac, the God in whom we believe is often the hidden God. The purposes of grace, liberation, forgiveness and healing are made present to us through the scandal of a vulnerable, sacrificial and bruised lamb. We could never have guessed that the destiny of the world could be bound up with the Galilean carpenter to whom John the Baptist pointed.

And yet this is New Testament faith. Preaching in Jerusalem on the day of Pentecost, Peter said: 'This [Jesus] was handed over to you by God's set purpose and foreknowledge; and you, with the help of wicked men, put him to death by nailing him to the cross. But God raised him from the dead, freeing him from the agony of death ... Exalted to the right hand of God' (Acts 2.23, 33). Later he also said: 'The God of our fathers raised Jesus from the dead – whom you had killed by hanging him on a tree.

God exalted him to his own right hand as Prince and Saviour' (Acts 5.30–1).

St Paul takes the theme further. In several of his letters, the exalted Christ, now at the right hand of God, is the one who is at the centre of this world's destiny. In Ephesians we read:

> In [Christ] we have redemption through his blood, the forgiveness of sins, in accordance with the riches of God's grace that he lavished on us with all wisdom and understanding. And he made known to us the mystery of his will, according to his good pleasure, which he purposed in Christ, to be put into effect when the times will have reached their fulfilment – to bring things in heaven and things on earth together under one head, even Christ (Ephesians 1.7–10).

To the Colossians, Christ is spoken of as the 'first-born of all creation', namely the uniting focus of all things.

The day is coming when Jesus Christ will be manifest to all creation as the leader and saviour of all. He is the Lord before whom every knee shall bow. He is the centre of the worship of heaven and earth.

The Lamb in the Book of Revelation

The book of Revelation celebrates this theme in a different way. It is written in a time of persecution, as an encouragement to the suffering churches to 'hang in there' and hold on in their faith. It describes, in vivid apocalyptic imagery, the world in terms of conflict between God and the powers of evil. It depicts the ultimate victory of God's Messiah and his judgement of the whole world order. It tells of the inauguration of a new heaven and a new earth, and of the gathering of every tribe and tongue and people and nation around God's throne.

And the centre of the worship of heaven and earth is a Lamb!

> Then I looked and heard the voice of many angels, numbering thousands upon thousands, and ten thousand times ten thousand. They encircled the throne and the living creatures and the elders. In a loud voice they sang:
>
> 'Worthy is the Lamb, who was slain, to receive power and wealth and wisdom and strength and honour and glory and praise!' (Revelation 5.11–12).

Twenty-eight times in the book of Revelation, the Lord Jesus Christ is given the title 'the Lamb'. Usually it is used in the context of his majesty and kingly rule

So to whom is the world coming? To Jesus Christ, the Lord, the Lamb who was slain, the king of glory. World history and world destiny come to their focus and fulfilment in him. When that day comes, 'righteousness and peace will kiss each other',[2] there will be no more inequities, no more tears, no more pain, no more death. In the kingdom of Christ's glory, creation itself is made whole.

What is remarkable in the book of Revelation is that, whereas in John's Gospel the Greek word used to speak of the Lamb of God is *amnos*, the writer of the book of Revelation chooses the word *arnion*. *Amnos* refers to the Lamb of sacrifice. The author of Revelation needs that plus something more. For here the Lamb is not only sacrifice, he is also ruler, warrior, victor. He is the Lamb who was slain; he is also the horned Lamb of Revelation 5.6 at the centre of heaven: 'Then I saw a Lamb, looking as if it had been slain, standing in the centre of the throne, encircled by the four living creatures and the elders.'

Where does this image come from?

Back to the Book of Enoch

To get our bearings, we need to go back once again into the Old Testament, and to growing expectancy that in the last days, God would send his Messiah. As far back as 1000 BC at the time of the death of King David, the great king of Israel, the people began to hope for another king like him: someone of power and prestige; someone under whose reign the nation would prosper and be safe from her enemies. But the nation went through many troubled years. The kingdom was divided into Israel and Judah. The nation's fortunes took a plunge downwards. Then came the conquests: the northern kingdom of Israel was overrun, and eventually the people of Judah in the south were taken away into exile.

After the exile, various prophets kept alive the hope of a new king, and after the close of the Old Testament period, the people of Judah still kept looking for a future new age of God. Some of the apocalyptic writings of that period between the Old and New Testaments reflect this. They point forward to a coming Messiah king. One of the vivid word pictures in the book of Enoch, for example (quoted by C. H. Dodd in *The Fourth Gospel*) is of the people of God as a flock and their leader as a sheep or ram. The great King David himself is represented as a lamb who becomes a ram, a ruler or leader of the sheep.

For example:

> But behold lambs were borne by those white sheep, and they began to open their eyes and to cry to the sheep ... and I saw in the vision how the ravens flew upon those lambs and took one of those lambs, and dashed the sheep in pieces and devoured them. And I saw till horns grew upon those lambs, and the ravens cast down their horns; and I saw till there spouted a great horn of one of those sheep ... and it cried to the sheep, and the rams saw it, and all ran to it ... and those ravens fought and battled with it and sought to lay low its horn, but they had no power over it ... and I saw till a great sword was given to the sheep, and the sheep proceeded against all the beasts of the fields to slay them, and all the beasts and the birds of the heaven fled before their face. (Enoch 15.6–19)

Some scholars think that the great horned ram depicted in this paragraph refers to the Maccabean revolt in the middle of the second century before Christ, led by Judas Maccabaeus against the Seleucid Empire which had conquered Palestine. Others take it to be a direct prophecy of the coming Messiah himself. Whatever the primary reference in the book of Enoch, this is exactly the sort of symbolism which is picked up centuries later in the book of Revelation. The vulnerable Lamb becomes the horned victorious one. The Lamb who was slain is the Lamb on the throne. In Christian understanding, Jesus (which means saviour) is Christ (which means Messiah), the Lord. In other words, although in the suffering and death of Jesus of Nazareth we see only vulnerability, the service of suffering love – such that some who had hoped that he would be proclaimed king of Israel were disappointed – in the exalted Christ of glory, Jesus ascended at the Father's right hand, we do see the king whose power and authority were expressed through that vulnerability and pain.

It will be important at this point to probe the use of the imagery of the Lamb in the book of Revelation a little further.[3]

Behold the Lamb

In the first place, we notice that the Lamb is described 'as if it had been slain' (Revelation 5.6). The Lamb is the redeemer, through whose shed blood men and women are set free. On the ground of his death, the great multitude which no man can number are able to wash their robes and make them white (Revelation 7.14). In Revelation 15.3, the song of the Lamb is linked with the song of Moses, the great deliverer at the Exodus. Here are echoes of the passover lamb which we were describing earlier in chapter 2. As the people of Moses' day celebrated their deliverance from Egypt, so the multitude of heaven sing the song of the Lamb.

Jesus, Lamb of God, have mercy upon us.

Second, the Lamb is at the centre of the peoples' worship. The vivid picture is drawn of the throne of heaven. The elders, the living creatures, all the redeemed men and women bow down before the Lamb, who is worthy of all worship (Revelation 5.8,12ff. 7.9–10). The Lamb shares the throne of honour with God.

Jesus, Lamb of God, we worship you.

Third, the Lamb is a ruler. He is 'in the centre of the throne' (Revelation 5.6). 'A throne speaks of order and administration; the wounded lamb on the throne of order restored by sacrificial death.'[4] The Lamb opens the seals of the book, and is proclaimed king of kings and lord of lords. His kingdom, as Hans Küng once put it, is creation healed.

Jesus, Lamb of God, we would obey you.

Fourth, the Lamb is the judge. Behind all the vagaries, the achievements, the grandeur, the guilt and the evil of world history there lies the operation of the kingdom of the Lamb. The book of Revelation unveils something of the workings of this divine kingdom on the stage of world history. The Lamb is also the judge before whom all are called to account. If we take the strange word 'wrath' to refer to the outworking in world history of the consequences of sin, then we can perhaps understand something of the terrifying phrase in Revelation 6.16: 'the wrath of the Lamb.' In him, evil is finally punished. For the Lamb standing before the throne is also the Lion (Revelation 5.5–6). His roar is the

inescapable judgement of God. In the worship of
heaven, everything which is disordered, broken,
polluted, evil and worthy of wrath will be either
mended or destroyed. The Lamb's all-seeing seven
eyes will no longer look on any evil (Revelation
5.6).

Jesus, Lamb of God, deliver us from evil.

Fifth, the Lamb is the provider. 'The Lamb at the
centre of the throne will be their shepherd' (Revelation 7.17). All life in heaven is lived in dependence
on the gracious sustaining, leading, providing Lamb.
Here, in a lovely mix of images, the Lamb becomes
the shepherd. The One who was slain is now the
resurrected and living One, who in great tenderness
cares for his flock. 'The Lamb at the centre of the
throne will be their shepherd; he will lead them to
springs of living water. And God will wipe away
every tear from their eyes.'

Jesus, Lamb of God, wipe away our tears.

Finally, the Lamb is the bridegroom. The bride is
Christ's Church (Revelation 21.9), and the marriage
feast celebrates the final victory of God over all the
powers of darkness. 'Hallelujah! For our Lord God
Almighty reigns. Let us rejoice and be glad and give
him glory! For the wedding of the Lamb has come'
(Revelation 19.6–7). In that day, the heavenly city
shall be established for all whose names are written
in the Lamb's book of life (Revelation 21.22). From
the throne of God and the Lamb flow the water of
life (Revelation 22.1), and his servants shall worship

him. 'They will see his face, and his name will be on their foreheads. There will be no more night. They will not need the light of a lamp or the light of the sun, for the Lord God will give them light. And they will reign for ever and ever' (Revelation 22.4–5).

Jesus, Lamb of God, grant us your peace.

He is the One to whom this world is coming; he comes to his world. And if this is what will be, how should we live now, that God's kingdom may come on earth as it is in heaven? He comes to us in grace: the Lord will provide. He comes to us in liberation: the Lord sets his people free. He comes to us in forgiveness: the Lord will restore. He comes to us in suffering: the Lord will heal. He comes to us in victory: the Lord reigns. Grace strengthens our faith, as it did Abraham's. Liberation frees us for obedience, as it did God's people on passover night. Forgiveness restores us through repentance, as the worshippers making their burnt offerings came to understand. Through suffering there is healing for growth and for completion, as Isaiah's suffering servant portrayed. God's victory over evil inspires our worship, for at the centre of heaven, is a Lamb.

So where are we in the book of Revelation? Perhaps we are among that strange collection of people on Mount Zion with the Lamb's name on their foreheads, of whom it is said 'These are they who follow the Lamb wherever he goes' (Revelation 14.4). The whole of Christian discipleship could be summed up in that phrase. God give us grace to follow the Lamb wherever he goes.

For Further Reflection

Between them and the foot of the sky there was something so white on the green grass that even with their eagles' eyes they could hardly look at it. They came on and saw that it was a Lamb.

'Come and have breakfast,' said the Lamb in its sweet milky voice.

Then they noticed for the first time that there was a fire lit on the grass and fish roasting on it. They sat down and ate the fish, hungry now for the first time for many days. And it was the most delicious food they had ever tasted.

'Please, Lamb,' said Lucy, 'is this the way to Aslan's country?'

'Not for you,' said the Lamb. 'For you the door into Aslan's country is from your own world.'

'What!' said Edmund. 'Is there a way into Aslan's country from our world too?'

'There is a way into my country from all the worlds,' said the Lamb; but as he spoke his snowy white flushed into tawny gold and his size changed and he was Aslan himself, towering above them and scattering light from his mane.

'Oh, Aslan,' said Lucy. 'Will you tell us how to get into your country from our world?'

'I shall be telling you all the time,' said Aslan. 'But I will not tell you how long or short the way will be; only that it lies across a river. But do not fear that, for I am the great Bridge Builder. And

now come; I will open the door in the sky and
send you to your own land.'

C. S. Lewis, The Voyage of the Dawntreader, 1952

Jesus! the name high over all,
In hell, or earth, or sky;
Angels and men before it fall,
And devils fear and fly.

Jesus! the name to sinners dear,
The name to sinners given;
It scatters all their guilty fear,
It turns their hell to heaven.

Jesus! the prisoner's fetters breaks,
And bruises Satan's head;
Power into strengthless souls it speaks,
And life into the dead.

O that the world might taste and see
The riches of his grace;
The arms of love that compass me
Would all mankind embrace.

His only righteousness I show,
His saving grace proclaim;
'Tis all my business here below
To cry: Behold the Lamb!

Happy if with my latest breath
I might but gasp his name;
Preach him to all, and cry in death:
Behold, behold the Lamb!

Charles Wesley (1707–88)

Notes

Introduction

1. G. T. Manley and H. W. Oldham, *Search the Scriptures: A Three Year Bible Study Course* (InterVarsity Fellowship, 1949), p. x.

Chapter 1

1. Nicholas Wolterstorff, *Lament for a Son* (Eerdmans 1987; Hodder Spire 1988).
2. Gerard W. Hughes, *God of Surprises* (Darton, Longman and Todd, 1985).
3. This phrase is borrowed from the title from Jean-Pierre de Caussade's book, *Self-Abandonment to Divine Providence*, tr. Algar Thorold (Burns and Oates, 1933).
4. C. S. Lewis, *Voyage to Venus* (Bodley Head, 1943).
5. 1 Corinthians 15, especially verses 35 to 44.
6. Peter Forster, 'Providence and Prayer' in T. F. Torrance (ed.) *Belief in Science and in Christian Life* (Handsel Press, 1980), p. 110.
7. David Atkinson, *The Message of Ruth* (InterVarsity Press, 1983), p. 43.
8. Frances Young, *Can These Dry Bones Live?* (SCM Press, 1982).
9. Young, *Can These Dry Bones Live?* p. 48.

Chapter 2

1. Erich Fromm, *The Fear of Freedom* (Routledge, 1942)
2. See Amos 3.2; Hosea 8.13; 12.13; Micah 6.4; etc.
3. Karl Barth, *Church Dogmatics* II/1 (T & T Clark, ET 1936–), p. 386.
4. This is a term from falconry: to engraft feathers in a

damaged wing so as to restore damaged powers of flight.
From J. N. Wall Jr. (ed.), *George Herbert* (Paulist Press,
1981), p.157.
5. This verse alludes to Acts 12.1–11.

Chapter 3

1. John Calvin, *Institutes of the Christian Religion*, Book III.
19.7
2. G. J. Wenham, *The Book of Leviticus*, The New International Commentary on the Old Testament (Eerdmans,
1985), p.51ff.
3. R. C. A. Hunter, 'Forgiveness, Retaliation and Paranoid
Reactions', *Canadian Psychiatric Association Journal*, 23,
1978.

Chapter 5

1. Gustav Aulén, *Christus Victor* (SPCK, 1970).
2. See Psalm 85.10
3. I am drawing heavily on a paper by N. Hillyer ' "The
Lamb" in the Apocalypse', in *EQ*, XXXIX/4, 1967.
4. Hillyer, ' "The Lamb" in the Apocalypse'.